1998

Successful Team Management

ESSENTIAL BUSINESS PSYCHOLOGY
Series editor: Clive Fletcher

This series interprets and examines people's work behaviour from the perspective of occupational psychology. Each title focuses on a central issue in management, emphasizing the role of the individual's workplace experience.

Other books in the series:

The Healthy Organization
Ethics and Diversity at Work
Sue Newell

Business Leadership
Viv Shackleton

Impression Management in Organizations
Paul Rosenfeld, Robert A. Giacalone and Catherine A. Riordan

The Psychology of Personnel Selection
Dominic Cooper and Ivan T. Robertson

Innovation and Change in Organizations
Nigel King and Neil Anderson

Successful Team Management

Nicky Hayes

INTERNATIONAL THOMSON BUSINESS PRESS
I ⓣ P An International Thomson Publishing Company

London • Bonn • Boston • Johannesburg • Madrid • Melbourne • Mexico City • New York • Singapore • Tokyo • Toronto • Albany, NY • Belmont, CA • Cincinnati, OH • Detroit, MI

Successful Team Management

Copyright © 1997 Nicky Hayes

First published by International Thomson Business Press

I(T)P A division of International Thomson Publishing Inc.
The ITP logo is a trademark under licence

British Library Cataloguing-in-Publication Data
A catalogue record for this book is available from the British Library

First edition 1997

Typeset in the UK by J&L Composition Ltd, Filey, North Yorkshire
Printed in the UK by Clays Ltd, St Ives plc

ISBN 0–41511–409–8 (Paperback)
ISBN 0–41511–408–X (Hardback)

International Thomson Business Press
Berkshire House
168–173 High Holborn
London WC1V 7AA
UK

International Thomson Business Press
20 Park Plaza
13th Floor
Boston MA 02116
USA

http://www.itbp.com

To my nephew Nicholas
with my love

Contents

— *Figures*

— *Tables*

— Boxes

Note
Each of the organizational examples discussed in these boxes has
been drawn directly from real-life. Inevitably, therefore, this has
meant that the companies or organizations concerned cannot be
named, and so pseudonyms have been used. The few exceptions
occur when the organization concerned has already given permission to be named in previously published material which forms
a source for the discussion.

— Series editor's preface

The rapid, far-reaching, and continuing changes of recent years have brought about a situation where understanding the pyschology of individuals and teams is of prime importance in work settings. Organizational structures have shifted radically to the point where individual managers and professionals have far greater autonomy, responsibility and accountability. Organizations seek to reduce central control and to 'empower' individual employees. Those employees combine in teams that are frequently cross-functional and project-based rather than hierarchical in their construction. The traditional notion of careers is changing; increasingly, the expectation is that an individual's career is less likely to be within a single organization, which has implications for how organiztions will command loyalty and commitment in the future. The full impact of the information technology revolution is finally being felt, with all the consequences this has for the nature of work and the reactions of those doing it.

The capacity of people to cope with the scale and speed of these changes has become a major issue, and the literature on work stress bears testimony to this. The belief in the importance of individuals' cognitive abilities and personality make-up in determining what they achieve and how they can contribute to team work has been demonstrated in the explosive growth in organizations' use of psychometric tests and related procedures. Perhaps more than ever before analysing and understanding the experience of work from a psychological perspective is necessary to achieve the twin goals of effective performance and quality of working life. Unfortunately, it is the latter of these that all too often seems to be overlooked in the concern to create competitive, performance-driven, or customer-focused cultures within companies.

It is no coincidence that the rise in the study of business ethics and increasing concern over issues of fairness paralleled many of the organizational changes of the 1980s and 1990s. Ultimately, an imbalance between the aims and needs of the employees and the aims and needs of the organization is self-defeating. One of the widely recognized needs for the years ahead is for a greater emphasis on innovation rather than on simply reacting to pressures, yet psychological research and theory indicate that innovation is much more likely to take place where individuals feel secure enough to take the risks involved, and where organizational reward systems encourage experimentation and exploration – which they have signally failed to do in the last decade. Seeking to help organizations realize the potential of their work-force in mutually enhancing ways is the business challenge psychology has to meet.

The aim of the *Essential Business Psychology* series is to interpret and explain people's work behaviour in the context of a continually evolving pattern of change, and to do so from the perspective of occupational and organizational psychology. The books draw together academic research and practitioner experience, relying on empirical studies, practical examples, and case studies to communicate their ideas. Hopefully, the reader will find that they provide a succinct summary of accumulated knowledge and how it can be applied. The themes of some of the books cover traditional areas of occupational psychology, while others will focus on topics that cut across some of those boundaries, tackling subjects that are of growing interest and prominence. The intended readership of the series is quite broad; whilst they are most directly relevant for practitioners, consultants, and students in HR and occupational psychology, much of what they deal with is increasingly the concern of managers and students of management more generally. Although the books share a common aim and series heading, they have not been forced into a rigid stylistic format. In keeping with the times, the authors have had a good deal of autonomy in deciding how to organize and present their work. I think all of them have done an excellent job; I hope you think so too.

Clive Fletcher

1 *Why use teams?*

INTRODUCTION

To an ever-increasing extent, modern management has become focused on the idea of the team. Management consultants propose organizational restructuring to facilitate teamwork, directors make policy statements about the importance of the team to the organization, and senior managers exhort their junior staff to encourage teamworking in their departments. Where organizational culture became the managerial buzz-word of the 1980s, teamworking became the managerial concept of the 1990s.

And with reason. Teams have enormous potential. A growing number of organizations have found that changing to team-based work has had far more far-reaching effects than anyone could have predicted. In industry, directors report that both production levels and profits increased and their company improved its sales and marketing strategies when it went over to teamwork. In the public sector, tasks are reported to be performed more thoroughly and efficiently, jobs become enriched as more direct contact with clients or patients becomes possible and team members offer one another support in coping with difficult situations. In all types of organization, whether public or private, reports indicate that teamworking improves staff morale and decreases staff turnover.

These are powerful claims and indeed, there are those who claim even more. For example, Katzenbach and Smith (1993) argue that high-performing organizations depend on the creation of strong, semi-autonomous working teams. They see other approaches to management as counter-productive, and even damaging, on the grounds that ultimately, all they do is to lead the organization into static practices and eventual stagnation. A chief executive aiming to lead a dynamic organization, they argue, should forget about hands-on management. Instead, that CE should set up structures and systems which will allow teams of people to take the organization's running into their own hands.

Box 1.1   **What is teamwork?**

The idea of teamwork is not always an easy one to grasp. Most organizations, after all, organize their work-force into groups of people who work together but each have their own jobs to do; and these are often referred to as teams. But simply having an arrangement whereby people work together isn't the same as having an organization which has converted to teamwork.

Essentially, the message of teamwork is delegation and empowerment. Teamworking is all about passing responsibility over to working teams, so that they can get on with what they have to do without continually having to refer to higher levels in their organization. That means that the teams need to be given enough authority to make day-to-day decisions about their work and enough power to make sure that things are done properly.

Many inexperienced managers – and also many who ought to know better – feel that they have to keep control of everything that happens in their organization or department, so they are reluctant to allow employees the power to make decisions on their own. Yet over-control of that kind can create a tremendous amount of damage. The people who know their jobs best are the people who are actually doing them; and they are often able to see what needs doing much better than those at higher levels of management. Moreover, it is often difficult for people to communicate freely with people in authority over them, so managers often don't realize what problems are caused when their decisions are inappropriate.

Although some managers see the idea of teamwork as threatening their own jobs, in fact it does quite the opposite.

It is the manager who has to make the overall, strategic decisions which will help to keep the organization or department on course. Managers represent their department at higher levels and initiate wider-reaching projects, such as training initiatives, which their employees might not realize are possible. And, most importantly of all, managers are the people who make it possible for the team to get on with its work: who are available with support when needed and who can discuss with the team its direction and goals. So managers actually do a great deal – but what they *don't* do, in a teamworking structure, is run the day to day work. They rely on the team to do that.

Teamworking, then, is very different from the old-fashioned, high-control, authoritarian management that is still, unfortunately, so common. But it is also much more effective. Organizational psychologists have known for a long time that when people are given responsibility, they act in a much more responsible way. Strict, authoritarian systems produce resentful and passive employees and interfere with communication into the bargain. But teamworking gives people a sense of being valued and we all work better when we feel that our efforts are appreciated. Teamworking also encourages people to be more professional in their approach and to take their responsibilities seriously. All of which is a tremendous benefit to any organization.

That doesn't mean, of course, that teamworking is the answer to all ills. As Guest (1995) pointed out, organizational change requires interventions at several different levels within an organization: not just at the level of the working group. When the Rover Group transformed its management practices – and hugely increased its profitability and market share – teamworking was just one type of change out of many changes to the organization as a whole (see Table 1.2). But it was teamworking which involved the organization's employees directly and which created a situation where everyone could work together to help the company to succeed. Teamwork allows a company to draw on the ideas and potential of their people, so that it can build firmly on its strengths.

Management may be subject to fashions, but organizations don't make such radical changes just on a whim. According to Katzenbach and Smith, directors and senior management are turning to teamwork for one reason and one reason only: because when it works, it works very well indeed. They cite numerous examples of organizations which have been entirely transformed – for the better – by changing their practices in this way. In an organization which has got its teamwork practices right, people work more efficiently, experience less stress and contribute more to their work. They stay with the company longer and don't take as much time off sick. They contribute new ideas and try to improve the way that they do their work. The result is that the organization functions better internally, saves money and becomes more competitive.

Not every organization which introduces teamworking finds these effects, of course. Some companies have introduced teamworking and found that it hasn't really made much difference at all. But it is clear that if it is implemented well, teamworking does make a dramatic difference. For an organizational psychologist, this raises a number of questions. Why should working in teams make any difference? Why does being organized into autonomous (or nearly autonomous) working groups affect people's motivation? And how might understanding the psychological processes underpinning teamwork help managers to manage their teams more successfully in real life?

About this book

This book covers many areas: team-building, team leadership, how teams can influence their organizations and so on. When we actually look into the psychology of teamworking, we find that working in teams taps into some very deep-rooted mechanisms in human psychology. The roots of these mechanisms lie far back in our evolutionary past, but they are very real and very powerful influences on everyday life. As we explore the different aspects of teams, teamworking and team management, I hope that these mechanisms will become clearer. If we can understand why successful teams can be so powerful, then we are in a better position to establish positive teamworking ourselves.

Knowing why, however, is only part of the process. We also need to be able to see what it means in practice so that we can understand it fully. To this end, each chapter in this book contains a number of case studies, which give real-life illustrations of some of the examples given in the chapter. The case studies are all taken from real organizations and describe situations which have happened in the recent past. There are probably as many examples of bad practice as of good, because we can all learn from other people's mistakes. But for that reason – to prevent embarassment to the individuals or companies concerned – I have used assumed names for the organizations concerned. The exceptions occur where the case study was drawn from previously published research, for which the company concerned gave permission for its name to be used.

Seeing examples of other people's practice can help our understanding of the issues, but we also need to be able to translate that understanding into practical action. It's one thing understanding that a manager should be fostering a positive sense of identity among the work-force; but a manager also needs to know just how that can be done. Because of that, I have introduced a set of management recommendations at the end of each chapter in this book. These are intended to show how the implications of each chapter can be translated into practice: to provide practical guidance for managers who would like to develop their skills in this area.

The idea, then, is that this book should allow its readers to explore and examine the different aspects of successful team management. That exploration needs to include why teams work in the way that they do, but also how teams can be managed to ensure that they work as effectively as possible. Obviously, though, the book deals with team management in general and every organization is different. So the important thing is to understand the fundamental principles of team management and how they work. Knowing those principles will help any manager to develop an appropriate teamworking strategy for their particular company, organization or department. Successful team management should be a practical reality, as well as an idealistic aim.

TYPES OF TEAM

We often use the word 'team' quite loosely. But teams can take many different forms and serve many different functions. In

Chapter 2, we'll be exploring some of the differences between the team and the working group; but here we will look at some of the different types of teams which can be found in organizations.

Production or service teams

The type of team which most commonly comes to mind when we think about teams in organizations are those teams which are actively involved in manufacturing, production, or service. They include teams of stewardesses or stewards on aircraft, production-line assembly teams involved in direct manufacturing, mining or drilling teams, computing or data processing teams and maintenance teams such as those involved in municipal gardening or building maintenance. Essentially, their work is routine and it is involved in keeping up a steady flow of production or services.

Teams of this type usually consist of full-time workers, who may sometimes have worked together over many years. These teams are largely self-managing in terms of the rest of their organization, in that they organize their own work and get on with it. How far individual team members have a say in what they do, though, is usually up to the team manager, who is also the link between the team and the rest of the organization.

Action/negotiation teams

Another type of team consists of highly skilled individuals who come together to engage in special activities where each person's role is clearly defined. These teams include surgical teams, musical groups, sports teams, airline cockpit crews and military combat teams. These teams tend to be entirely task-focused, with each team member having specific skills which contribute to the successful performance of the task. So it is the task which the team has to perform which effectively defines how the team members operate.

Since the tasks which these teams perform are complex and sometimes unpredictable, it is vital that each team member is able to draw from their own expertise to contribute to the whole. That way, it is possible to improvise in unusual situations. The role of management in these teams is really about establishing the task or mission which the team has to perform. Once that has been done, the team takes over. Within the team itself, leadership is not about directing individual activities. Instead, it is mainly concerned with co-ordination and timing.

Project and development teams

Product development teams, research teams and project teams form a third type of team. These teams tend to operate across a much longer time span: they can sometimes take years to complete a particular development project, such as the design of a new type of car or computer. Sometimes, these teams have come together for a single project and the team members go on to different work once their task is completed. Sometimes, though, they are ongoing, permanent teams with a general research role in the organization. Whichever type of lifespan they have, these teams tend to consist of highly skilled technical or professional people, with a mixture of different specialisms. They tend to organize their work internally and will often have a reasonably high level of autonomy, in respect to the rest of the organization.

Advice and involvement teams

The fourth type of team is concerned with providing organizational advice and decision-making. High-level management teams are the classic example, of course, but this category also includes specialist advisory teams such as personnel or financial planning teams. Not all of these teams are at high levels in an organization, though: this category can also include quality control circles and employee involvement groups, whose role is to generate ideas, advice and to pass on suggestions.

Most advice and involvement teams have a fairly restricted scope, and don't take up a great deal of working time – their members have other roles within the organization. At the lower levels in the organization, such teams often don't have all that much autonomy, although that depends to a very large degree on the organization's commitment to teamwork. In some organizations – notably the Japanese-run companies – teams of this kind have a very high priority. Not surprisingly, it is those organizations which tend to be featured in management articles extolling the successes of teamworking.

There are other kinds of teams, of course, but these represent the most common kinds of teams which we encounter in organizational life nowadays. Sundstrom, de Meuse and Futrell (1990) looked at research into the various types of team and in particular at four variables: how highly differentiated the team members were from the rest of the organization; how much the team worked with other members of the organization (which they called integration); what the team's work-cycle was like, and the typical types of outputs made by each type of team. Their findings are summarized in Table 1.1.

Table 1.1 Types of teams and their differences (adapted from Sundstrom, de Meuse and Futrell 1990)

Type of team	Differentiation	Integration	Work cycle	Typical Outputs
Advice/ involvement (e.g. boards, committees, councils)	Low	Low	Variable: either brief or long	Decisions, selections, suggestions, recommendations,
Production/ service (e.g. cabin crews, manufacturing teams, maintenance teams)	Low	High	Repeated or continuous processes	Manufacturing, processing, retail sales, customer services, repairs
Project/ development (e.g. research groups, planning teams, working parties, task forces)	High	Low	Variable: often one cycle is team's life-span	Plans, designs, investigations, reports, prototypes, presentations
Action/ negotiation (e.g. sports teams, musical groups, expeditions, surgery teams, negotiating teams)	High	High	Brief performance events, often repeated under new conditions	Competitions, matches, expeditions, concerns, surgical operations, missions

What makes a good team?

There is some consensus in the management and organizational literature about the characteristics of a good team. A good team has a clear sense of itself as a special group, but its members are also able to interact positively with other people in the organization. The team as a whole cultivates and negotiates positive assumptions and beliefs among its members, which help them to operate effectively within their organization. They communicate clearly with one another and effectively with the rest of the organization. And working together, the team is more effective than those same people would be if they were working as individuals.

Some team managers appear to know how to foster these mechanisms instinctively. They are able to operate intuitively to encourage positive team qualities, and to head off destructive or counter-productive events. Other, equally good, team managers have had to learn how to manage their teams effectively. And part of learning how to do it involves understanding some of the mechanisms which are important in making teams work.

Innovation, kaizen and employee involvement

It is a truism to say that Japanese management procedures have always been more people-centred than Western ones. Japanese practices have a very different philosophical and social history, with some very different assumptions embedded in them. One of them, for instance, is that they are simply not as hung up on status distinctions as Western managers are, and that comes from their different cultural background.

In Europe and America, traditionally, those who worked hard were at the bottom of the social ladder. Achieving higher standing in society went with having a more comfortable lifestyle and also with having more leisure time. Those at the top of the social heap didn't work at all and, in Europe at least, those who were associated with trade or commerce were regarded as being of inferior social status. To gain social acceptance in the higher levels of European society, successful industrialists had to spend a lot of time trying to show how 'gentlemanly' they were, and how unlike their employees.

In traditional Japan, however, there was a much more egalitarian attitude to hard work. Although there were differences in

Box 1.2   **Quality circles and task groupings**

Teams can be dramatically productive. But that doesn't mean that any working group will automatically become an effective team, or that teams can simply be created and left to their own devices. One of the best examples of this comes if we look at the kind of team known as the Quality Control Circle, or sometimes just Quality Circle. The story of Quality Circles shows how a teamwork practice can be either more or less successful, depending on how it is implemented, and the type of context in which it is operating.

Quality Circles have an interesting history. They originated in another wave of insights into the idea that if people are treated like people, then they can take responsibility and will rise to it, which took place in America in the 1950s. As part of this wave, many companies developed systems by which employees were encouraged to make suggestions about improvements to the company. This idea was exported to Japan as part of the post-war reconstruction liaison between that country and America. There, it became transformed into the Quality Circle. Quality Circles began as study groups for employees to look more deeply into the manufacturing processes, but increasingly began to tackle practical problems which arose in the workplace. Groups of employees took on responsibility for quality control, dealing with problems and identifying weaknesses. It is estimated that something like three million Japanese workers are involved in some kind of official Quality Circle.

In the early 1980s, as a result of a revived interest in Japanese management practices, the idea of the Quality Circle was re-exported to America and thence to Western management circles in general. It was adopted enthusiastically by many companies, because it seemed as though this would provide the key to the extremely high quality of Japanese industrial output.

In many companies, the practice proved to be very successful. Kanter (1983) described how Hewlett-Packard introduced 'quality teams' and found that in six months the teams managed to improve efficiency across the company by 50%.

They had given their supervisors 40 hours of training and then let them find their own way of implementing the concept among their work-force. The team members rapidly became involved in this aspect of their work, committed and productive.

In other companies, though, the picture was less rosy. Quality Circles were introduced following the step-by-step plans and procedures laid out in the textbooks and articles, and failed to engage the work-force. Instead, employees quickly became cynical and apathetic about the point of the exercise and the Quality Circle movement as a whole became regarded as just another managerial fashion. Except in Japan, of course, where they continue to be as positive a force as ever.

Some would say that this example shows how pointless it is to attempt to root up practices embedded in one culture and transplant them to another. Certainly, the Japanese practice is deeply embedded in its culture, and particularly in the working philosophy of *kaizen*, of which more later. But the Hewlett Packard experience shows that such 'cultural borrowing' is not impossible. What doesn't work, though, is to attempt to implement a procedure which involves human beings as actively as this, in a step by step policy followed from a management manual. Treating people like cogs in a machine is hardly the way to bring out their constructive side!

social status, it wasn't centred around working – everyone was expected to work hard, no matter what their social station. So industrialization brought with it a readiness for a very different approach to high-level management – not one which was based on imitating the leisured classes, but one in which all, including those at the top, were expected to contribute wholeheartedly to the enterprise, for the good of all.

As a result, Japanese firms rarely go in for the ritualistic distinctions of dress, office space and dining rooms, which are so common in Western ones. Instead, all employees, no matter what their status, will eat in the same canteen, may wear the same kind of company overalls and are regarded as each contributing in their own way to the enterprise as a whole.

So when it comes to instituting voluntary working teams acting for the good of the company, such as Quality Circles, Japanese companies are operating within a very different climate. It is automatically assumed that everyone has something to contribute and that it is worth listening to what the work-force has to say. In Western companies, by contrast, it is often extremely difficult to get management to acknowledge that their work-force may have anything to contribute. So the attempts they make to harness those contributions are half-hearted and their employees are quick to detect that they don't really mean it.

Kaizen

Another advantage which Japanese companies have is that Japanese industry, for the most part, is based on a philosophy known as *kaizen*. Imai (1986) described *kaizen* as an overriding emphasis on continuous change and improvement, as a contrast to the Western idea of innovation. Innovation, Imai argued, is seen by Western organizations in terms of a single, one-off set of major changes, which will result in improved operating procedures or working practices. Once these are in place, working life is expected to run along smoothly under the new system.

Kaizen, by contrast, is the idea that working life is a continuous process of change and development. Small improvements are being made to the system all of the time and even the tiniest improvements are incorporated into the company's way of working. By contrast to the 'steady-state' model of organizational life which is implicit in the Western concept, working practices are in a state of continuous development and everyone in the organization is involved in contributing to it.

Against this type of background, it's easy to see why Quality Circles became such a huge feature of Japanese industrial practices. If an improvement in working practice is something which is out of the ordinary, and has to have a managerial decision made about it, people are going to think twice about making the suggestions – if only to ask themselves whether it is really worth the trouble. But if improvements in working practice are happening all the time, a suggestion becomes much easier to make: it's less of an issue. So Japanese companies which aim to involve their work-force in suggestion-making and improvements are doing so in a much more positive cultural climate.

That doesn't mean, though, that all Western companies are the same. In Chapter 6 and elsewhere (Hayes 1991), I have discussed how organizational cultures can be seen as social representations – shared beliefs and assumptions held by members of working groups and by organizations as a whole. I'll be exploring the implications that this has for team management in Chapter 6. But it is worth noting that one organization, in the same line of business, may hold a very different set of social representations than another.

Some Western companies, for example, independently developed working practices which are very similar in essence to the Japanese ones. IBM, for example, started out that way from the beginning. When Thomas J Watson Jr founded the company, back in 1914, his goal was to achieve lifetime employment for its staff. Naturally, that meant learning how to use those human resources to the full and IBM really did manage to develop systems which treated their people as the company's most valuable resource. And an important element in that was the way that they used working teams constantly, and very effectively, as well as utilizing and encouraging suggestions from their work-force.

Some companies, such as the Rover group in Britain, managed a full-scale transition of their culture from an old, authoritarian (and strike-ridden) hierarchical system to one which consciously involved the work-force in day to day decision-making, and tried to do away with the old status barriers. Bower (1994) described the critical success factors in this process (see Table 1.2) and discussed the way that much of the transformation was achieved by re-organizing the work-force into self-managing teams, which could take responsibility for their sector of the organization's work. Rover's new approach proved outstandingly successful, turning the company from one which was on the brink of collapse to one which was highly profitable in a very competitive market.

So it can be done. Organizations can change, they can develop new ways of operating and they can re-structure themselves successfully so as to make the most of their human resources, regardless of the common assumptions of their culture. Teamworking can make a tremendous difference in this. But adopting such policies has to be serious: the history of the Quality Circle shows us that trying to adopt these methods as superficial 'quick-fix'

Table 1.2 Critical success factors in the Rover Group transition (Source: Bower 1994)

During its transformation, the Rover Group adopted the following aims:

We must:

1. Create a culture which provides purpose, dignity and recognition to every individual in an environment of trust which is open, safe and secure.
2. Help the leaders by empowering and supporting them in pursuit of company goals.
3. Achieve world class resourcing standards, ensuring we have the right people in the right numbers with the right skills, in the right places at the right time – right first time.
4. Create continuous learning with development opportunities for everyone and sharing of best practice.
5. Ensure company-wide understanding of the compelling business needs by maintaining continuous dialogue.
6. Empower individuals and teams to achieve success through commitment, motivation, flexibility and skills development.
7. Foster positive involvement relationships with the broader Rover community.

---

techniques, or mechanistically by following step-by-step instructions, isn't enough. If we are to use teams effectively, we need to understand why they work, and how.

PSYCHOLOGICAL DIMENSIONS OF TEAMWORK

Whatever type of team it is, a team consists of a number of individual people working together to achieve a common goal. Simply because they are human beings, this means that teamwork involves psychology – and quite a lot of it. Effective communication, for instance, draws on body language as well as choice of words and metaphors. If we tried to analyse every single psychological aspect of teamworking, we would soon get bogged down in a mass of detail, and for this reason I don't propose to do that in this book. I shall, however, discuss psychological processes when they become important for understanding some aspect of how teams work. In the section on decision-making, for instance, I shall be describing some of the psychological mechanisms which operate in that sort of situation.

But there are some over-arching psychological mechanisms which permeate the whole process of working in teams. These are absolutely central to why human beings work well in teams at all and if we really want to understand what is going on, we need to look at them carefully. I shall describe the basics of these psychological mechanisms in the rest of this chapter, because I will be referring to them again quite often throughout this book.

The two psychological mechanisms which are particularly helpful when we are trying to understand the psychology of teamwork are known as social identification and social representations. Put in its simplest form, **social identification** is our human tendency to see the world in terms of 'them-and-us' – to see ourselves as located in various social groups, which are different from 'the others'. **Social representations** are the shared beliefs or assumptions which we pick up from others and adjust until they fit into our own personal beliefs and opinions. That's probably the simplest way to describe them. But as with all simplifications, that misses out on a lot of rather important detail: they each need a bit more explanation.

Social identification

Human beings are deeply social animals and modern human society consists of many different groups. Each of us belongs to several social groups: large-scale ones, like gender or social class categories; medium-scale ones, like jobs or professions; smaller-scale ones like clubs, families or interest groups. At different times, belonging to one category rather than another can become an important part of how we see ourselves. In one context, you might describe yourself as a gardener or a skier; on another occasion, you might describe yourself as a manager or a psychologist and on a third you might describe yourself as a parent.

Each of these labels represents a social group and provides us with a social identity. Because they are real parts of our own identities and not just acts, each of them also has its own set of thoughts, ideas and attitudes. We can switch very quickly from one to another – and we do, if it becomes relevant. Often, all it takes is for someone to say something about 'you golfers' in a conversation. Instantly, the other person switches into 'golfer mode' and the conversation is transformed from a simple inter-personal discussion into a confrontation between two distinct groups – 'them-and-us' – golfers and non-golfers.

Belonging to our different social groups is an important part of how we see ourselves – just as much as the self-image or self-esteem. In fact, dividing the world into 'them-and-us' seems to be a very basic mechanism in the human psyche – it's something that people do all the time and without realizing that they are doing it. Sometimes, those 'them-and-us' distinctions can be harmful, leading to misunderstandings and conflict. A lot of a manager's job can involve smoothing things out between different departments which can't communicate with one another because the 'them-and-us' barriers have become too strong. But sometimes social identifications can be positive, helping people to gain a clearer understanding of what they are doing and how they can go about doing it.

When psychologists were first researching social identity processes, it was assumed that 'them-and-us' groups would automatically be in conflict with one another. Early studies seemed to imply that the minute a distinctive group was formed, it would see itself as in competition with other groups of its kind. More recently, psychologists have found that such conflict isn't inevitable. Different groups and teams can work side-by-side, without seeing the others as the opposition. It depends on how the teams are managed.

Rivalry with other groups, in other words, is all about competition for resources. If two groups don't see themselves as being in competition for resources, it is easy for them to work together and co-operate. But if there is perceived competition – and the competition doesn't even have to be real, as long as the people concerned believe it exists – then the groups will each see 'the others' as being 'the opposition' and all our ancient 'them-and-us' awareness will come into play. Being distinct doesn't automatically mean being hostile to other groups: it depends how much the different groups really do have things to clash about, or how much they think they have.

Mechanisms of social identification

Psychologists who have studied the mechanisms of social identification have found that it stems from two very basic psychological processes. The first of these is classification. Social identity theory argues that it is fundamental to human perception to classify things. We see the world as consisting of buildings, vehicles, people, furniture and other 'types' of things – it's a lot easier that way. And we also, whether we are aware of it or not, classify people into 'types': managers, teenagers, BMW drivers, mums, businesswomen and so on. We automatically group people together in ways that make sense to us, in terms of our own understanding of how the world works.

But our understanding of how the world works also carries the implication that belonging to some social groups has more prestige or kudos than belonging to others. And this brings in the second fundamental psychological process which is involved in social identification. Essentially, we all like to be able to think well of ourselves: we are highly motivated to obtain positive self-esteem from the things that we are or do. So it is important to us that we can feel proud of, or good about, belonging to our own particular groups.

If the group that we belong to doesn't provide us with any kind of positive self-esteem, there are two things that we can do. We can leave the group or distance ourselves from it; or we can try to change how the group is perceived. Companies with excessively high turnover rates are often ones which are failing to provide their members with any opportunities for positive social identification. People like to be able to feel proud of the company they are working for and to feel that they are truly contributing to their organization.

Sometimes, though, we don't have a choice about leaving a group: if you need a wheelchair to get about, for instance, you are in the 'disabled' social group whether you like it or not. You might cope with that by distancing yourself, and saying that you're 'not like the rest of them' – in other words, by refusing to identify with that particular social group. Or you might join a group of high-achieving disabled people, or work to change the way that disabled people are perceived by society in general. All of these are ways that we can derive a positive sense of self-esteem while belonging to that particular social group.

Self-esteem at work
People, then, are very highly motivated to derive positive self-esteem from belonging to their particular social group. And this applies at work, as well as at home. But at work, belonging to a particular group also carries with it messages about the nature of our relationships with others – such as whether the person we are interacting with is superior or subordinate to us, whether these

interactions might have repercussions in our subsequent working lives, whether certain people are likely to have significant technical expertise which we should respect and so on.

As we've seen, without a positive source of self-esteem from their group membership, people will respond in one of two ways: they will either seek to detach themselves from the group, or they will seek to change the group's perceived status. These are familiar strategies in organizations: as we've seen, high staff turnover rates can often be traced to the fact that people can derive very little self-esteem from being employed to do that particular job; people may dissociate from their group ('well, yes, I do work in accounts but I'm not like the rest of them'), or they may re-define how important their particular job is ('we may not count for much, but they couldn't run the place without us').

Leaving some groups, of course, could represent a desirable course of action – it may be about achieving promotion and increased status within the organization. In organizations which offer realistic scope for promotion, people do not have to leave the organization in order to join a higher-status group; and this is another factor which can strengthen social identification. Knowing that you could move on up if you wanted to can make all the difference: belonging to a group from choice is very different from belonging to it because you don't have any option.

There are a number of other ways of allowing people to feel good about belonging to their working group. One of them is internal communication about the achievements of the organization itself and encouraging staff to be aware of their own contribution to those achievements. Another option is enhancing professionalism: developing internal and external training so that people are able to take a pride in their work and the way they go about it. That sort of professionalization tells employees that their management has sufficient belief in them to feel that such efforts are worthwhile and this too makes it easier for people to feel positive about their own working group.

Essentially, then, social identification shows us that people have a very fundamental tendency to see the world in terms of 'them-and-us' groups and that they are also highly motivated to feel proud of belonging to the group that they belong to. It is an ancient source of motivation, deriving from the fact that human beings are social animals; and teamworking taps directly into this source of motivation. Belonging to a team allows people to feel special – to feel that 'their' group is distinctive and competent. And by doing so, it also gives people a direct source of positive self-esteem, which motivates them to keep up the team's working quality and make sure that they continue to do well.

Social representation theory

People who identify with a social group also have a tendency to see the views or opinions of people in their group as more valid than the view of outsiders. Over time, members of a consistent working group get to know and understand one another's beliefs and although they still have different ideas and opinions, they often come to share a great many beliefs and assumptions about work and working life. These shared beliefs and assumptions are known as social representations.

Social representation theory was developed by the French psychologist Serge Moscovici (1984). It is all about the shared beliefs which are held by groups and cultures and the functions which those shared beliefs serve in day-to-day living. Social representations are really mini-theories, about what the world is like, about human nature and about how or why things do or don't change. They are used to justify our social actions and to explain why things happen the way that they do. And as any newcomer in an organization knows, such shared beliefs can form a powerful determinant of action, or inaction, as the case may be.

We don't swallow social representations wholesale: we negotiate them through conversation and discussion, until we have a version which we can accept and which we can integrate with our own existing beliefs and ideas. If they can't be adapted in this way, we reject them altogether. But often, what will happen is that we will accept some part of the social representation and adapt other bits of it. Conversation, according to Moscovici, is all about developing, adapting and negotiating social representations. As we talk to people, we are trying out different ideas and explanations and receiving other people's views. Eventually, we synthesize these into our own opinions and ideas.

Social representations aren't just abstract beliefs. They serve a function, allowing us to justify or rationalize our own preferences or actions. In other words, they are useful to the person who holds them. This is why we each develop our own set of social repre-

Box 1.3   **Social Representations In Practice**

I was once doing consultancy in two firms, which were both
in the same line of work and about the same size, although
their managerial practices were as different as chalk and
cheese. They were both small computer companies, mainly
involved with software development, and each of them was
about the same size, with between 20 and 24 employees.
They also had similar origins, each beginning with a small
group of individuals who had worked together in another
organization and had decided to try going it alone. As a
result, the directors tended to have a very high level of
computing expertise, but had been learning company management the hard way.

In one firm, referred to as 'Technocomp' – whose directors held almost classic Theory X beliefs about their work-
force – the working day began strictly at 9am and employees
were reprimanded if they arrived late. It ended at 5pm. Staff
who needed time off for personal reasons were expected to
take it from their holiday allowance. The directors' reaction
to a suggestion that they might become more relaxed about
timekeeping was to reply that their staff would only take
advantage of such 'weakness' and work fewer hours.

The second firm, 'Compusys' – whose directors held
Theory Y beliefs – had a much more relaxed approach.
Although the company's working hours were nominally
the same as Technocomp, there was little close supervision.
Nobody clocked in or out and nobody was reprimanded if
they were late. Instead, it was assumed that there was a good
reason for it and that they would make up the working time
that they had lost on another occasion – although no systematic check was kept of this either.

The differences produced by these assumptions were dramatic. I first became aware of them when I had occasion to
phone Technocomp at 8.30 in the morning – something I had
often done with Compusys – and found that nobody, not even
the directors, arrived until just before 9am. By five minutes
past 5pm, the whole office was deserted. No matter what

work anyone was doing, at five o'clock they downed tools and left. The staff kept strictly to their scheduled hours and no more.

The picture at Compusys couldn't have been more different. The working day began much earlier: their staff began arriving from 7.30am, and the directors were usually in by 8.00am. One employee even complained to me that 7.30am was too late and that they aimed to become a keyholder, so that they could arrive earlier! The working day also lasted longer, with many staff staying until 7pm or even later. If someone was working on an interesting project when the end of the day came, they would stay to finish it and many staff regularly worked more than their scheduled hours or came in at weekends to 'finish something off'.

The whole atmosphere in Compusys was one of confidence and goodwill: the directors had confidence in their staff and the staff had confidence in their directors. In an interview, one employee confided to me that his first weeks at the company had coincided with a messy and disturbing divorce. He had been told by the directors to take as much time off as he needed to sort things out and to make it up later, when he was more settled. At the time that I visited the company, three months later, he was voluntarily putting in a ten-or eleven-hour day, fully aware of how lucky he had been in his bosses and determined to repay them.

---

sentations, negotiated through our own thoughts and ideas. But even though we each have our own social representations, they still have a lot in common with those of other people. Social representations have a central nucleus, which doesn't really change and peripheral elements which we can adapt and adjust according to our existing personal constructs or ways of thinking.

Social representations often show up in behaviour, not in words: sometimes they are implicit, revealed by patterns of activity rather than by what people actually say. Jodelet (1991) showed how social representations about madness held by members of a French community were often revealed by actions rather than words. For instance, a family who were boarding someone diagnosed as schizophrenic might keep their eating utensils in a different place and wash them up separately. Their actions revealed a social representation about madness as potentially contagious, while their words did not.

The same thing can happen at work: people may say that they hold a particular view or policy, while their actions say something quite different. A company's directors may say, for instance, that they foster open communication and challenge from the staff, but the staff may be well aware that speaking out actually just brings trouble, or even the sack. So it isn't always possible to identify the social representations held in an organization simply by asking people what they believe. Often, we aren't really aware of our basic assumptions until we have an opportunity to stand back and analyse how we are acting.

Social representations, then, are generally accepted assumptions about reality which explain and make sense out of what is going on around us. They also reflect issues of power and social relations within their social context. They may appear through symbols, through words and images, or through actions, but really they are all about how social life, or working life in this context, operates. There is actually a considerable amount of organizational theory which deals with what social psychologists would recognize as social representations. The classic example, of course, is McGregor's Theory X and Theory Y, which we will look at later in this chapter.

Social representations and teamworking

Social representations aren't just relevant within the team itself. They are also fundamental to implementing teamwork properly in the organization. The idea of an organization which consists of self-regulating, dynamic teams is a far cry from the traditional model of organizational authority. In the traditional, centralized, organization the role of 'Head Office' is seen as ultimately determining every aspect of employment, including personnel policies, working procedures, purchasing decisions and industrial relations, while those at lower levels in the hierarchy simply get on with implementing those policies. Even when some responsibility for decision-making is delegated, a hierarchical structure still means that decisions must be made by those with a higher authority than those who are actually doing the work.

So shifting from a traditional, hierarchical organizational structure to a team-based organization is a very radical step and it involves big changes in the way that work is perceived. Management has always had its fads and fashions, it's true; but the type of transformation involved in shifting to a team-based approach goes much further than simply reshuffling chains of authority, such as adopting a matrix management structure or a new type of staff appraisal system. It actually means changing how power operates within the organization. And that involves a radical change of attitude.

The cornerstone of successful team management is respect. A team can't function as a team unless its members respect one another and it can't function well unless what it can do is respected by its management. Team members need to respect one another's skills and abilities; to respect their opinions and points of view and to respect their contributions to the overall tasks which need to be done. Without that basis of mutual respect, a team simply can't function well.

Ultimately, it is the team's manager who needs to set the tone of respect, communicating to the team that they are regarded as competent and capable. Managers who are mistrustful of their team members, or who override the team's decisions, or belittle the contribution of a given team member, are communicating something quite different and they are unlikely to achieve the levels of mutual respect and understanding which make for effective co-operation. No team can retain coherence if it is being subtly undermined by its manager. Equally, though, it is very hard for managers to maintain confidence if their approach is being constantly undermined by those above them.

Teamwork, after all, runs contrary to many established management practices, where traditionally it is assumed that the manager knows best and will direct the work of other people in the department. The transition from a centrally-controlled structure to a fully team-oriented one involved a very fundamental shift – in respect and also in trust. It involves a shift from the view that human beings need to be carefully watched and controlled and are liable to abuse any freedom they are given, to the idea that if people are given responsibility and autonomy, they will rise to it: if they are trusted, they will become trustworthy.

Theory Y, not Theory X

MacGregor would have found this familiar. As long ago as 1960, he was discussing the two different types of belief about human nature which different managers held. Theory X managers, he argued, took the view that people were shiftless, lazy and had to be made to work. Theory Y managers, however, saw people as basically hard-working and self-motivated, needing only to be put in a position where they were appreciated for these tendencies to become manifest.

More importantly, though, McGregor showed how these theories about human nature became self-fulfilling in the workplace. Theory X managers treated their people as if they were basically lazy and shiftless and in return their employees – or at least some of them – acted in that way. Theory Y managers treated their employees in a manner designed to communicate respect and belief in their abilities and in return experienced departments of hard-working, committed people.

These insights have been in the managerial literature for a long time. Wave after wave of managerial psychology has 'rediscovered' these insights and attempted to implement them. But the old-fashioned type of authoritarian control runs deep in our socialization: our educational systems, medical systems and social policing systems all rest on the idea that those 'underneath' must obey those 'in charge'. To shift from there to the idea that those 'underneath' can make their own decisions and that it is the responsibility of those 'in charge' to make it possible for them to do so, is a radical shift indeed. It requires a fundamental change in the social representations of work and working life held by all the members of the organization.

We can see, then, that the two psychological mechanisms of social identification and social representations are important in helping us to understand what is behind an effective team. Successful team management is all about drawing on these psychological mechanisms so that they can work to the benefit of the individual and the organization together. Teamwork challenges the alienation of modern living, providing people with meaningful interaction and shared sources of satisfaction at work. From our very earliest evolutionary origins, human beings have lived and worked in teams, pooling their efforts and sharing out tasks to make life manageable. Social identification runs very deeply in us:

indeed, it's more-or-less impossible to stop people from seeing the world in terms of 'them-and-us'. Teamwork harnesses that mechanism in a positive way and in doing so offers individuals a remarkably high level of personal and interpersonal reward.

SUMMARY

- Teams have a great deal of potential to contribute to modern organizational life. Positive working teams encourage flexibility, involvement and efficiency and the introduction of teamworking has been known to transform companies entirely.
- The four main types of team are: production/service teams, action/ negotiation teams, project/development teams and advice/involvement teams. Each type of team has distinctive characteristics.
- The story of quality circles shows that simply attempting to introduce teams mechanistically, without thought for the basic principles underlying them, is unlikely to be successful.
- The Japanese philosophy of *Kaizen* emphasizes continuous improvement and development, and helps to establish a culture in which employee involvement is fostered. Some Western firms have been able to establish similar organizational cultures.
- The two psychological mechanisms of social identification and social representations are both active processes underlying successful teamwork. Social identification has to do with 'belonging' to a group and social representation has to do with sharing fundamental assumptions or beliefs of the group.
- Social identification is a powerful force in successful team and organizational management. Feeling proud of their team or department and regarding it as special is intrinsically motivating for people, and does not require conflict or competition with other groups to be effective.
- Social representation theory is about the shared beliefs and assumptions which are negotiated through conversation and interaction as people work or live together. Managerial beliefs, as well as organizational cultures, can be seen as social representations which exert considerable power over organizational life.

Box 1.4   **Management recommendations**

Take a good, hard look at the way that your organization, company or department is functioning. Make a list of the parts of your organization's work which could be re-organized so that teams of employees could take responsibility for it.

Identify a group of people who could work as a team on a specific activity or project and bring them together for a discussion of teamwork possibilities. Encourage them to give their opinions freely.

Arrange communication mechanisms and activities to bring people together and give them a sense of belonging to the whole company or department.

Identify activities, events or communications which will encourage your people to be proud of belonging to their organization and make them happen.

2 *The team and the group*

INTRODUCTION

The idea of the 'team' at work must be one of the most widely-used metaphors in organizational life. A group of workers or managers is generally described as a 'team', in much the same way that a company or department is so often described as 'one big family'. But often, the new employee receiving these assertions quickly discovers that what was described as a 'team' is actually anything but. Instead, it's a group of people who are just getting on with their work – perhaps with a degree of job satisfaction and perhaps without. The mental image of cohesion, co-ordination and common goals which was conjured up by the metaphor of the team was entirely different from the everyday reality of working life.

It's a sporting metaphor, of course. The word 'team' sets up images of groups of athletes in a relay race, members of a football team ranged around the pitch; cricketers taking their turn to bat or combining to field. These images all carry the idea that different team members play different roles and all contribute to the overall outcome. The goalkeeper is as much a part of the football team as the striker, yet the activities of the goalkeeper are entirely distinct from those of the striker. Both players contribute to their team's success, but they do it by playing very different roles and having different responsibilities. The sporting team is a powerful image. But for many people, it is as far removed from the mundane reality of organizational life as the training and dietary habits of the athlete are from those of the population at large.

In some organizations, though, true teams really do happen –
and by a 'true' team I mean a group of people who are task-
focused, co-ordinated, each contributing their own personal
talents and abilities and energies to the job in hand. As we've
seen, the organizational literature abounds with accounts of how
the efforts of particular teams have transformed organizational
practices and profits. These accounts go across the board, ranging
from railfreight companies to newspapers, from photographic
industries to computer software houses, from insurance companies
to car manufacture. The stories are true, not exaggerated. A good
organizational team can achieve organizational and commercial
tasks which seem to be virtually impossible. Sometimes, organizational teams can completely out-perform expectations, produce
achievements which go way beyond anything which they, or anyone else in the organization, had envisaged at the beginning.

Such teams, though, are a far cry from the more mundane
reality of the 'team' in working life. What is often called a
'team' is, typically, a group of people working together – amic-
ably enough, but without co-ordination, common objectives and a
sense of teamwork. Strictly speaking, it is a working group rather
than a team and this is quite an important distinction. In this
chapter, we will be looking at some of the differences between
a team and a working group. And, of course, we will be looking at
some of the psychological mechanisms which are involved in the
whole process of group dynamics and of teamwork.

GROUP AND TEAM PROCESSES

Interest in working groups and work teams has very deep roots in
the history of organizational research. Organizational researchers
have known for some time just how influential working groups
can be. Their interest began in the 1930s, with the famous
Hawthorne Studies, conducted between 1924–27 by Elton Mayo
and his colleagues Roethlisberger and Dickson, at the Hawthorne
Works of the Western Electric Company in Chicago. Prior to these
studies, it had been assumed that people worked hard or didn't
work hard purely to maximize their own profit or gain. What
Mayo's research team showed, however, was that how hard
people worked was also influenced by human factors: whether

management was showing an interest, whether people felt they had some control over their working conditions and so on.

Group norms

In one distinctive case, though, the social factors identified by Mayo and the others had made very little difference to productivity. That set of workers had established a set of group norms which simply didn't change. The case is described in Box 2.1. In their reports, Mayo and the others argued that the bank-wiring room showed how working groups would always tend to develop their own norms and values, if they worked together for long enough. Other evidence from their research also supported this idea. Effective management, Mayo argued, should aim to manage these groups in such a way that the organization could benefit directly from the norms and practices evolving in its working groups. Ignoring them simply left them free to develop in such a way as to conflict with managerial goals instead.

These observations led to a considerable amount of research into group norms. Researchers found that, for the most part, group norms develop unconsciously and through force of habit. They emerge from the assumptions and beliefs that group members hold about the nature of their work; from the implicit expectations which are communicated from management to the group members about how responsible or otherwise they are; from the practicalities of the situation that they are working in and from a host of other similar factors.

Group norms are intangible and often difficult to express in words, but that doesn't mean that they are not real. People who belong to groups often try very hard to conform to their group's norms – because the price of failure may be exclusion from the group, or even ridicule. Both of these are very powerful motivators for human beings – we hate to appear ridiculous in front of other people, and we also hate to be left out or ignored. So the fact that the group is able to impose these **sanctions** – punishments – on members who don't conform means that group norms can be a powerful way of controlling people's behaviour.

Changes to group norms

Group norms don't always stay the same, of course. There are some cases where they do – working groups have been known to

Box 2.1   **The Bank-wiring room**

The set of studies conducted by Mayo and his colleagues, Roethlisberger and Dickson, investigated a number of different sections of the Hawthorne plant. Among their investigations was one part of the company in which the production rate was remarkably steady – it didn't go up, even when working conditions were changed by researchers, but it didn't go down either. This area was known as the 'bank-wiring room'.

There were fourteen men working in the area and their jobs involved attaching wires to switches which would become components of telephones. The investigation showed that these fourteen men had developed a close group, with its own established group norms to which everyone was expected to conform. From direct observation, and from interviews with each of the men, Mayo was able to isolate four distinctive principles which were very powerful determinants of the way that the men went about their work. These were:

1 Group members should not turn out too much work.
2 Group members should not turn out too little work either.
3 Group members should not tell anyone in authority anything which might get a colleague into trouble.
4 Group members should not try to maintain social distance or act officiously over other group members.

These four principles set the standards for group behaviour and ensured that the people working in that part of the company were able to maintain a steady rate of production, without either increasing or decreasing their productivity. The norms which the group had developed were strongly supported by the people working in that room, who resisted any external attempts to manipulate their productivity levels.

(Source: Mayo 1933)

maintain norms and traditions that have been passed on through several 'generations' of the work-force – but these are becoming less common in the modern world. Most working groups nowadays have experienced some changes to their norms and working practices. Sometimes, these changes are an unconscious response to changes in management expectations or organizational climate. And sometimes they are a deliberate response to a perceived market threat or organizational necessity.

Changes to group norms don't happen easily, though, and deliberate changes are hard to implement – as many managers have found to their cost. Indeed, it's open to question whether group norms can ever be changed from the outside: effective changes to group norms appear to happen only when the pressure comes from group members themselves, as individuals who can see the need for change gradually band together within the group to oppose the established norms and establish new ones. We can really only understand this if we are aware of how group norms are useful to the people who share them.

Functions of group norms
Feldman (1984) identified four entirely different purposes which group norms can serve – and each of them helps to ensure positive, consistent social action among the group members. The first of Feldman's norm functions is the way that group norms express the central, most important values of the group. By doing this, they allow group members to have a strong sense of what the group is all about, which they can use for directing their own behaviour as well as for relating to people outside of the group. They also help to define clearly what the group is not about – to distinguish between the type of activity which is acceptable to the group and that which is not.

Another important function of group norms is the way that they help the group to continue functioning smoothly, by establishing common ground and making group members' behaviour more predictable. Since everybody in the group knows what to expect, group members are able to set aside uncertainties in that respect and get on with the job in hand. This saves a considerable amount of cognitive appraisal and checking for social acceptability, and helps to streamline the way that the group operates.

A third function of group norms is the way that they help the group to define what is appropriate social behaviour among its members. This helps people to avoid embarrassing or difficult interpersonal situations, such as remarks which might hurt someone's feelings or make a group member feel ridiculous. In this way, the group is able to avoid confrontations or events which might challenge or threaten the co-ordination of the group as a whole and the group members are able to operate within a relatively 'safe' psychological environment.

The fourth function which Feldman identified was the way that group norms can sometimes help a group to survive, by helping it to maintain its distinctiveness and by rejecting any deviant behaviour shown by its members when it is under threat. (Like people, groups which feel secure are often much more tolerant of the occasional norm-breaking or deviance of its members, but a group which feels threatened or challenged can come down very strongly on a group member who breaks any of its norms). By protecting its special character, group members can feel more confident of their own roles as well as that of the group itself.

Pivotal and peripheral norms
That doesn't mean, though, that everyone in a group is obliged to act in exactly the same way. Schein (1988) showed how working group norms are effectively of two kinds: **pivotal norms** and **peripheral norms**. Pivotal norms express the most important, core assumptions about the nature of the work: for instance, a pivotal norm for someone belonging to an academic department might be that they expressed belief in the value of scholarship and education, whereas pivotal norms for a sales team might be that they should not alienate or offend a potential client. Peripheral norms, though, are less crucial, dealing with minor issues such as lunchtime practices, or how to seek information. Schein observed that a group will often tolerate quite a lot of deviation from its peripheral norms, while deviation from its pivotal norms is regarded much more seriously.

Schein went on to look at how people relate to their organizations and how that links with their conformity to pivotal or peripheral norms. Some people are reliable, unexciting organization members who conform to all of the norms. Some people conform to pivotal norms, but reject peripheral ones if they don't suit them. These people, Schein argued, are the creative individuals who make things happen within the organization. Other people accept peripheral norms but not pivotal ones, and these are in a state of what Schein described as 'subversive rebellion'; while a fourth set of people, who reject both sets of norms, are pretty well in open rebellion with the organization. In other words, Schein argued, the way that people contribute to the organization as a whole is closely linked to the way that they relate to the organization's norms.

Schein's classification, though, deals with the norms of the organization as a whole rather than with the type of norms which evolve in working groups. The influence of the organization as a whole is something that we will be looking at in Chapter 6, when we look at organizational cultures. In terms of working group norms, though, the question of whether an individual accepts or rejects group norms is more difficult, partly because of the way that so many people find it extremely difficult to challenge group ideas openly. Because we are social animals, disagreeing with other people face to face is something which most people find hard to do – even when they know personally that they are right and the rest of the group are wrong. It's a well-known psychological finding, which is summarized in Box 2.2. And what it means is that it can be difficult to observe directly how far people really do share their working group's norms.

Team norms
As we have just seen, one of the most important functions of group norms is the way that they define what the group is all about to its members. And it is here that we can find one of the key differences between a working group and a team. A team has norms, just as much as a group does – after all, a team is a kind of group, just a rather specialized one. The key difference lies in what the group's norms actually are – how they define what the group is about.

Sometimes, group norms may have little or nothing to do with the tasks which people are undertaking. 'Canteen cultures' and subcultures within organizations may have values which are very different from the organization as a whole and new employees may find themselves having to conform to norms which are very different from those which they envisaged before joining the organization. For the most part, though, working group norms

Box 2.2   **Conformity**

One of our strongest psychological tendencies when we are dealing with other people face-to-face is the way that we prefer to avoid confrontation. Most of us really don't like to stand out against the group, or to oppose other people's views, and this is made even more extreme when those other people are of higher status than we are and may react negatively to being challenged. Asch, in 1956, showed that even in situations where everyone was equal, someone who was put in the position of knowing that the rest of the group had not told the truth would often fail to speak out.

In Asch's experiments, people were asked to take part in an experiment which involved judging the lengths of lines. They were shown into a room with half a dozen other people, who they also believed to be experimental research participants. Each person was asked to say, in turn, which of three lines was the longest. The others all, one-by-one, gave the wrong answer, before the real participant was asked to speak. As a result, the real participant became increasingly anxious at the idea of confronting the group and often also gave the wrong answer as well.

Venkatesan (1966) found a similar result from a study which involved the participants selecting the 'best' suit from three identical alternatives. When people were asked individually, they were equally likely to choose any of the suits. But when they were asked with others present, who had already expressed a preference, the research participants all chose the suit which had been singled out by the others. Moreover, they held to this choice even when the others were not present and insisted that their chosen suit was different from the other two.

Of course, we don't always conform to other people. When Asch's study was repeated in 1980 by Perrin and Spencer, the researchers found that their modern participants – who had been drawn from engineering and medical students and believed that accurate measurement was important – were much more likely to stick to the truth. But they still became extremely distressed at having to do so. Going against a majority view – particularly if it is the view of people you identify with or feel you belong with – is a very difficult thing for a human being to do. The power of group norms is very real and it is even more relevant for a committee or group at work than it is in a psychological laboratory.

generally assume that people are there to do a job and include the shared value that members of the group should get on with their own work.

A working team, though, has rather a different set of values. Instead of assuming that each individual has their own job to do and should get on with it, a team's values contain the idea that the team has a shared task and that each individual's work is a direct contribution to the whole project. So everyone's work is seen as directly affecting everyone else's and this creates the climate for the emergence of a different set of group norms.

Team norms tend to be task-focused, valuing activities and practices which encourage efficient or thorough work and sanctioning activities which reduce efficiency or quality. They encourage task-oriented interactions, so that intervening to help someone out, or consulting with other team members as to the best way of doing something, is seen as ordinary working activity rather than exceptional. And they contain the idea that many different types of contribution are valuable to the task's completion. Instead of rejecting someone with different skills as 'not one of us', as a working group might, a team is more likely to value someone with different skills, as being able to bring different insight and expertise to bear on the main task.

So team norms and ordinary working group norms are quite different, even though they use the same psychological mechanisms in exerting their pressures. In particular, team norms tend to be oriented towards what needs to be done, so that social interactions, beliefs and assumptions and, above all, values are all working to make sure that the task which the team has to do is done well.

Group and team cohesion

Being in a group isn't the same thing as feeling we belong in a group. Group cohesion is the invisible bond which links members of a group or team together, so that they see themselves as 'belonging' to it and as different from 'the others' – group norms are an important part of what makes a group cohesive. There is some evidence that highly cohesive work groups are more productive than groups which are not particularly cohesive. For example, Keller (1986) studied working groups in American research and development organizations. The groups were organized around particular research projects and varied quite a lot in terms of how cohesive they were, but the highly cohesive groups were much better at meeting the task objectives which they had been set.

Apart from group norms, Piper et al. (1983) showed that one of the most important facets of cohesion is the attractiveness of the group to its members. People who belong to highly cohesive groups like their groups and enjoy belonging to them. Piper et al. also showed that such people are highly motivated to remain in their group and will often resist leaving quite strongly, if that becomes necessary (Piper et al. 1983). Much of the resistance to organizational restructuring has been shown to arise from the disruption of cohesive work groups and the way that people resist such disruption as much as they can.

It has often been argued that management can be more effective if it is able to draw on these mechanisms positively, to enhance working life. In the 1960s and 1970s, several proposals for effective management structures (e.g. Likert 1967) were based on the idea that management should structure their organizations so that their basic units consisted of consensual, autonomous working groups. This was based on the idea that if the group were cohesive, then positive working norms and working practices would evolve more or less automatically. So a number of techniques for establishing group cohesion emerged, such as the use of sensitivity training exercises, t-groups and encounter groups. Some of these (although not all) are also useful for building teams, so we will be looking at them in Chapter 3.

In Japan, group cohesion is recognized as a very important factor in working life, and nurturing group cohesion among their workers is seen as one of the prime responsibilities of Japanese managers. Japanese managers are expected to pay a lot of attention to establishing a positive working group, and to work with their subordinates to maintain morale and enthusiasm. Hodgetts (1991) reported that this emphasis on group cohesion produced a number of positive effects, including low levels of absenteeism, low staff turnover and a high degree of employee involvement in working practices.

Organizational research into group cohesion has turned up several different factors which can be important in promoting group cohesiveness. McKenna (1994) listed seven of these, which are given in Table 2.1. That doesn't mean, though, that all group cohesion is equally effective, or equally desirable from a managerial point of view. There are such things as canteen-cultures and groups with different beliefs and goals from the organization as a whole. As we can learn from the Hawthorne bank-wiring room

Table 2.1 Factors in group cohesiveness (adapted from McKenna 1994)

Similarity of attitudes and goals	This usually means that people enjoy being in one another's company.
Time spent together	This provides the opportunity to explore common interests and ideas.
Isolation	This can produce a feeling that the group is special and different from others.
Threats	These emphasize the importance of interdependency and can cause the group to solidify, though they do not always have that effect.
Size	Smaller groups are more cohesive than larger ones, partly because their members interact with one another more.
Stringent entry requirements	Having to overcome hurdles to get into a particular group strengthens identification with that group, because of the cognitive dissonance which would be produced otherwise.
Rewards	Incentives based on group rather than individual performance produce a group-centred, co-operative perspective among members.

study, if a cohesive working group is to be effective it is important
that the group's goals are in line with the goals of management.

Team cohesion

If we want to use the mechanisms of group cohesion to build
effective working teams, then what we really need to know is
how, and why, group cohesion develops in the first place. In
psychological terms, this is all about the process of social identification. In the last chapter, we saw how people automatically
divide the world into 'them and us' groups, and how we like to
belong to groups which reflect positively on our self-esteem. What
is described as group cohesion in organizational textbooks is all to
do with the sense of belongingness, which comes when we identify ourselves with a particular social group.

Recognizing that social identification is the mechanism which
underlies group cohesion puts us in a much better position if we
are trying to understand the principles of successful team management, because it helps us to understand what makes an effective
working team. At the end of the last chapter, I mentioned how
three features of social identity theory – classification, group
cohesion and positive self-esteem – have particular implications
for team management. It's easy for a manager to assign individuals to a team. But it's quite another thing getting that group of
people actually to function as a team, and establishing cohesion is
an important part of it.

Cohesion, though, doesn't depend on similarity – even though
early research into social identity seemed to suggest that it did.
It's important that a team is able to see itself as distinctive and
special, but that doesn't mean that everyone has to be perceived as
identical. In fact, when we identify with a particular group or
team, it is 'outsiders' who we see as similar, not 'insiders'. To
put it in its crudest form: 'we' are all different, but 'they' are all
the same. A cohesive group is able to tolerate quite a lot of
differentiation among its members – sometimes even more than
it regards as acceptable from others. Marques and Yzerbyt (1988)
showed that we are reasonably likely to tolerate a 'black sheep' in
our own group. But if we find the same deviant behaviour in an
'outsider', we regard it as unacceptable.

In a working team, the members may have very different skills,
professions, responsibilities and even status. So there is no reason

to assume that the different team members will see themselves as being similar. Indeed, the whole point of a team is that it brings together and co-ordinates people with different skills, so that the team's tasks can be carried out as effectively as possible. The important thing is that the team members should have a clear understanding of the way that each of them contributes to the team's efforts as a whole – and for that, we need effective communication.

Does distinctive clothing help?

One question which is sometimes raised is that of whether it is helpful for a team to have special clothing, presenting a common identity between team members. The question has arisen because of the way that common company 'uniforms', have sometimes been so dramatically successful, particularly in high-powered manufacturing companies. When the Rover Group transformed its working practices so dramatically, both the management and the work-force adopted the new company overalls. It might seem a trivial thing, but it was a visible sign of unity within the car manufacturing plant, which worked very well.

That isn't to say, though, that it would have worked without the many other changes which the company implemented, which we looked at in Chapter 1. The reason that the 'company uniform' could be effective was because it became a visible symbol of a number of other practices: if it had been introduced on its own it would have been extremely unlikely to be effective. Moreover, it was introduced in a company which had a visible and single manufacturing identity which could bring the work-force together – everyone in the organization was ultimately concerned with manufacturing cars, no matter what their particular job was. The adoption of company overalls was both symbolic of unity and symbolic of the process of car manufacture.

What we can learn from Rover and from similar examples, is that the whole question of company clothing, or company uniforms, is inextricably linked with company practices. A uniform is inevitably a symbol: the uniforms of police officers, hotel doormen, nurses and traffic wardens each hold symbolic meaning for all of us. Uniforms also differentiate between individuals of different status: uniforms in hospitals, for example, make very precise statements about the role and position of the individual wearing them and these statements reflect the tightly hierarchical divisions of health care practice.

In many companies, of course, uniforms are used to differentiate those members who deal with the public from those who are higher in the management scale and tend to work behind the scenes. There are, of course, advantages to promoting a consistent public image, particularly in a service industry: the uniform of a McDonald's assistant is known pretty well everywhere and serves as a global marketing device to promote the image of the organization as a whole. But those companies which adopt this type of approach also have to make serious attempts to ensure that these status divisions do not interfere with information flow and organizational communication within the organization. Since the uniform emphasizes the difference between management and workforce, the management needs to try very hard to maintain a sense of company unity and to ensure that it does not result in 'them-and-us' barriers between management and work-force.

Whether a company uniform is a unifying force, promoting social identification with the company, or whether it acts to reinforce differences in status as it does in hospitals, depends entirely on the underlying context which the uniform is symbolizing. Some multidisciplinary health care teams, for example, have found it a positive benefit to ensure that nobody wears uniforms to their team meetings. The team members still bring their professional expertise to the meeting, of course, but they have found that their team's discussions flow more freely and are less hampered by irrelevant or unnecessary barriers if the visible signals of their professional groups are absent.

For the most part, in most companies, it is unlikely that a company uniform would produce many benefits. Where the uniform also symbolizes the core business, as in Rover, then it can be valuable as a statement about what everyone has in common. The work of most organizations, though, is much more diverse, or is extremely difficult to symbolize. In those organizations, any attempt to introduce common clothing would be more likely to produce resentment among the staff than to promote any active sense of unity. Fostering social identification with an organization requires a rather more subtle approach than the adoption of a particular style of clothing.

The same applies within teams. What promotes a sense of unity in a successful team is the shared information and the knowledge that the whole team is acting co-operatively to get things done. Clothing cannot establish that: the best it can do is to symbolize it and that isn't really necessary for the team members themselves. What team clothing can do, though, is to establish barriers between the team and other people working in the organization. It's a statement which says: 'these people are different', and that can be a real disadvantage at times.

Of course, there can also be times when that differentiation is useful. One can envisage a situation in a manufacturing industry, for example, where a team might be mingling with the rest of the work-force but have particular responsibility for attending to matters of safety, or quality control. Having a visible sign that someone belongs to that team could be helpful to the rest of the work-force in the same way that the uniform of the policeman or St. John's Ambulance member is helpful. But if the team's task depends on positive interactions and open information exchange with the rest of the organization, then the disadvantages of having a group easily identifiable as 'them' and not 'us' will usually outweigh any advantages of special clothing.

The importance of communication
Communication is probably the single most important factor for establishing cohesion among team members. It is vital to make sure that each team member realizes how every other person contributes to the task which the team has to do. That may sound obvious, but often working teams involve people at very different levels of the organization – which means that the team manager's attitude is crucial. A manager who believes that lower level employees don't 'need to know' information isn't likely to be able to perform well in a team. A manager who respects the contribution of each team member, regardless of their formal organizational status, will be in a better position to nurture task-oriented group norms and a sense of pride in membership of the team.

Effective communication between team members does more than simply remove status barriers. Because everyone is aware of what is going on, people can share pride in their team's achievements, concerns about setbacks, anxieties about meeting deadlines. They are in a good position to help one another out, or to put in extra efforts when it becomes essential – and they are able to do this voluntarily, simply because they can see for themselves that it is needed. All of these factors help the team to maintain a sense of cohesion – of belonging together.

If an organization is to benefit fully from the team's efforts, then it is also important to make sure that there are clear avenues for communication to pass outwards from the team to the rest of the organization. This can be achieved formally, through reporting-back sessions or regular e-mail bulletins, as well as informally, through social events, cross-departmental training events and the like. In many organizations, it is often the informal friendships developed by cross-departmental or cross-team contacts which provide the most reliable sources of information and serve to counteract or minimize inaccurate rumours.

Even when the information is stated frankly, though, effective communication can still be difficult to achieve. Misunderstandings can develop, or someone can mean one thing but be misinterpreted as having meant something entirely different. Part of the reason for this lies in our own individual psychology – in the personal constructs which we use to make sense out of our experience. We each have a well-developed set of personal constructs (see Box 2.3), which we have built up from our own experience over time, and these can often lead us to misinterpret or misunderstand what we are being told.

A successful team manager, therefore, needs to be sensitive to the different personal constructs which the team members hold and to take these into account when misunderstandings occur. The personal constructs held by someone who has come, say, from the production line are likely to be entirely different from those of someone who has come from the research team – and different again from someone who has come from personnel. The result can be either a strength or a weakness: it can result in clashes and misunderstandings, or it can provide a reservoir of different perspectives and specialist knowledge.

As we can see from Box 2.3, knowing about the way that people use personal constructs also carries an important message about delegation. Effective team leaders need to make sure that their team members understand just what it is they should be doing something about, how it works and why it matters – but then they need to let the team members go from there. That way, they and

Box 2.3   **Personal constructs**

The theory of personal constructs was developed by George Kelly, a clinical psychologist, in the 1950s. Kelly was particularly interested in how we make sense out of other people's behaviour and in the way that the same event can be interpreted quite differently, depending on who is doing the interpreting. Personal constructs are relevant for work too: look at how people respond to a suggestion made by their manager about a different way of working. Some people will respond to the suggestion with a 'let's try it and see how it works out' kind of attitude. Others, though, adopt a more suspicious approach and go for the 'there's some unpleasant ulterior motive here' interpretation.

The reason for these differences is in the **personal constructs** that people hold, about their working situation and about that manager in particular. We all have our own set of personal constructs: mini-theories which we use for understanding our everyday lives. We develop them by acting like scientists: forming hypotheses to explain why someone did what they did, testing them out, changing them if they don't seem to fit and so on. Our personal set of constructs has been built up over a long time and encapsulates an awful lot of experience. So someone whose experience has led them to develop personal constructs which imply that managers will always look for ways of getting their pound of flesh at the expense of the work-force isn't going to change their mind overnight. But given time, and in the right working environment, they will change it eventually.

Whenever we are interacting with other people at work, we are fitting whatever they say into our own personal constructs of how the company should work, what their work-force is like and so on. This means that we select bits from what the other person says – the bits that we think make sense, or are relevant – and ignore the rest. Moreover, if we have accepted some overall goal, such as a production target, or some kind of innovation, we immediately bring our personal constructs about the organization into play and use these to judge whether it is practical or not.

It applies to management too. When I'm doing consultancy, I never give directors or managers step-by-step instructions about what, exactly, they should do. That would be pretty pointless, since they are going to fit whatever I say into their own personal constructs of how the company should work, what their work-force is like and so on. This means that they are likely to select some of what I have said – the bits that make sense to them – and ignore anything which doesn't fit. I bear in mind that it is the managers who are in the company every day, while I am only there for a short time. This means that their personal constructs and anticipatory schema about what is practical for their people will be more sophisticated than mine – they will know more about the ins and outs and fine details of organizational life.

But I also know that it is hard to get an overview of your own department or company and to appreciate the underlying psychological mechanisms which are operating. In addition, my own training and professional knowledge has given me insights into the situation which they don't have. So I focus on making sure that the managers or directors I am dealing with can integrate the central messages into their own construct systems: that they understand the underlying problems and principles such as how the psychological mechanisms work, why they ought to do something about it and what it is that they are ultimately aiming to achieve. I might also provide a few examples of different ways of reaching the same goals. But by leaving the precise step-by-step decisions to the people who will have to implement them, those directors are in a better position to act effectively – not just now, but in the future as well.

the team can harness all that intelligence and thinking – all those human resources – instead of expecting people to act like robots.

Roles and skills

For a long time, researchers into group processes have been interested in the different roles played by group members. As long ago as 1948, the organizational researchers Benne and Sheats drew up a list of different group roles, which reflected the different contributions which individuals could make to their group. Their typology was fairly complex, and involved three major categories. The first of these categories was 'task roles' and these were to do with how the group went about dealing with its particular task or problem. The second category was 'group-building and maintenance roles', which were concerned with maintaining group cohesion and positive social interaction. The third category was what the researchers called 'self-centred roles'. This dealt with the way that some people use roles on committees or in other groups to serve their own personal interests. The full set of roles developed by Benne and Sheats is given in Table 2.2.

If we look at the list in Table 2.2, we can see immediately that these roles are meant to describe how people go about interacting with their group. They are not about individual characters, or overall styles, but about what is going on during the course of a meeting or event. In this classification, it is open to people to adopt whichever roles appear to suit that particular moment: even though any one person might adopt a habitual role, they might sometimes adopt others and end up playing a different part in what the group was doing at the time.

Unfortunately, however, since the roles were described as if they were 'character parts' in a play, it was all too easy for managers and other researchers to assume that Benne and Sheats were actually describing consistent roles which would be adopted by single individuals, rather than how the same individuals might act from moment to moment. Partly as a result of this confusion and partly because of the strong influence of psychometric tests, the concept of role became seen as almost interchangeable with the concept of personality type – although the two are really very different.

This problem led to the emergence of two different strands of group research. One approach focused on how interpersonal interactions take place in the group: looking at styles of intervention and approaches to social interaction. Although some of these eventually proved to be a bit of a dead end, they did have an influence on organizational research and we will be looking at them in Chapter 3. The second approach continued to explore group roles, but in a way which saw them as consistent features of the individual's personality, rather than as acts, or dramatic

Table 2.2   Roles in working groups (adapted from Benne and Sheats 1948)

Group task roles

Initiator-contributor	Recommends new ideas about, or novel solutions to, a problem
Information seeker	Emphasizes facts and other information from others
Opinion-seeker	Solicits input concerning attitudes and feelings about ideas under consideration
Elaborator	Clarifies and expands on the points made by others
Co-ordinator	Integrates information from the group
Orientor	Guides the discussion and keeps it on the topic when the group digresses
Evaluator-critic	Uses some set of standards to evaluate the group's accomplishments
Energizer	Stimulates the group to take action
Procedural technician	Handles routine tasks such as providing materials or supplies
Recorder	Keeps track of the group's activities and takes minutes of meetings

Group building and maintenance roles

Encourager	Encourages others' contributions
Harmonizer	Tries to resolve conflicts between group members
Compromiser	Tries to provide conflicting members with a mutually agreeable solution
Gatekeeper	Regulates the flow of communication so that all members can have a say
Standard setter	Sets standards and deadlines for group actions
Groups observer	Makes objective observations about the tone of the group interaction
Follower	Accepts the ideas of others and goes along with the group majority

Self-centred roles

Aggressor	Tries to promote own status within the group by attacking others
Blocker	Tries to block all group actions and refuses to go along with the group
Recognition seeker	Tries to play up their own achievements to get group's attention
Self-confessor	Uses group discussion to deal with personal issues

Self-centred roles

Playboy	Engages in humour and irrelevant acts to draw attention away from the task
Dominator	Attempts to monopolize the group
Help-seeker	Attempts to gain sympathy by expressing insecurity or inadequacy
Special interest pleader	Argues incessantly to further own desires

parts which a person might choose to play if the situation seemed to require it.

Team roles

More recently, the emphasis of organizational research in this area has shifted from the concept of the working group to the team. The shift was a subtle one, with the difference not really being spelled out particularly clearly. But, as we've seen, one of the main features of the distinction is that the idea of the team includes the idea of a group of people who are primarily task-directed: where the working group is a set of people whose work keeps them in regular contact, the team is a set of people who have a specific task and are working together in order to achieve it.

As research interest shifted into the idea of the team, interest in group roles made a transition to that of team roles. Belbin, in 1981, proposed a set of eight significant roles which, according to Belbin, were the core of an effective decision-making team and which were also essential in other kinds of teamwork in organizational life. These roles are listed in Table 2.3. A recent revision (Belbin 1993b) changed the name of 'chairperson' to 'co-ordinator' and 'company worker' to 'implementer', although the role descriptions themselves remained essentially similar.

Belbin arrived at these roles through a series of simulation exercises, in which managers attending management development courses were asked to work in groups to analyse the implications of particular case studies. By combining individuals with different attributes, Belbin showed that successful teams consisted of a mixture of different individuals. Moreover, Belbin argued that successful teams would always, of necessity, involve people playing different roles: a team in which nobody acted as 'plant',

Table 2.3   Team roles (adapted from Belbin 1981)

Role	Activites	Characteristics
Chairperson	Clarifies goals and objects; helps allocate roles, responsibilities and duties; articulates group conclusions	Calm, average intellect, trusting, impartial, self-disciplined, positive thinker, self-confident.
Shaper	Seeks patterns in group discussions; pushes group towards agreement and decision-making.	High-achiever, highly strung, impatient, outgoing, argumentative and provocative, dynamic.
Plant	Advances proposals and offers new ideas; gives new insights on courses of action.	Individualistic, serious-minded and knowledgeable, unorthodox, intellectual.
Monitor / evaluator	Analyses problems and complex issues; assesses the contributions of others.	Sober, clever, discreet, detached, unemotional, not easily aroused.
Company worker	Transforms talk and ideas into practical activities.	Tough-minded, practical, tolerant, conscientious.
Team worker	Gives personal support and help to others.	Gregarious, sensitive, team-oriented, indecisive.
Resource investigator	Introduces external information; negotiates with outsiders.	Curious, versatile, sociable, innovative, communicative.
Completer	Emphasizes the need for meeting schedules and targets, and completing task.	Perfectionist, perseverance, conscientious, attention to detail, anxious

generating new ideas, would not be successful; and nor would one in which nobody acted as 'completer'.

Although Belbin did accept that some people might be able to play more than one role, he also argued that effective management would need to ensure that all of these roles were covered in a given team – if necessary, 'importing' someone to play a part if it wasn't already being played. That suggestion reveals quite a change of emphasis: rather than being a temporary stance which reflects the demands and issues of the moment, the concept of role had become transformed into the idea of a consistent pattern, relevant for all working groups, and tied to particular individuals. Unfortunately, this shift of emphasis severely weakened team role theory as it developed, since it then became unable to cope well with individual flexibility.

A further development of the idea of group roles came with the idea of the 'Team Management Wheel' put forward by Margerison and McCann (1991). Their eight specific roles are grouped into four general approaches: explorers, advisers, controllers and organizers. Within these approaches are eight different roles, which overlap the general category rather than falling neatly into them. The roles include reporting and advising on relevant information, promoting the team to outsiders, innovating and creating new ideas, assessing and developing those ideas, organizing the team's activities into coherent stages and objectives, concluding (ensuring that projects are carried out fully), controlling and inspecting the quality of work produced by the team, and upholding or maintaining the social and organizational relationships within the team. As you can see from Figure 2.1, in this model, it is the linker who co-ordinates the various team members and activities and also acts as the team's representative with 'outsiders' – in other words, who gives the whole set-up a degree of coherence.

While it is clear that a successful team does involve different contributions from the participants and while it is equally clear that different roles may be crucial to the overall success or otherwise of the team, tying the role to the individual is much more contentious. Much of the experimental evidence supporting the idea of team roles has derived from a relatively narrow range of research situations: for example, Belbin provided each group with case studies and asked them to use the information to solve a particular problem. Although the content of the case study and of the problem varied, the task itself was essentially pretty consistent. So it may not be surprising that the managers concerned acted in reasonably consistent ways.

The problem, though, is that a very different situation may bring an entirely different facet of personality to the fore. People act in different ways in different situations. One person may take the role of 'shaper' with respect to one type of task, while adopting an

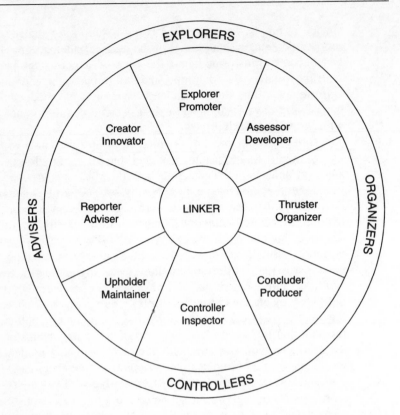

Figure 2.1 The team management wheel (source: Margerison and McCann 1991)

evaluative role in another, and a 'plant' role in a third. It depends on expertise and knowledge, as well as on personality inclinations. In a team where people are working positively and efficiently together, the role which they play at any one time will depend as much on the nature of the immediate task, and the skills which it requires, as it does on the other members of the team. Of course, people are likely to adopt consistent areas of responsibility but the whole point of a strong team is that it is able to bring out other abilities and resources in its members.

The assumption that people can be categorized into 'types', and that they will always tend to act consistently as a result, is one which has dogged organizational research for many decades.

Indeed, it is the assumption behind many recruitment policies, especially at higher levels in organizations. But there are social dimensions to how people interact with one another too and each of us will adjust our behaviour to the social situation in which we find ourselves.

One of the consistent puzzles in the organizational literature is the way that a high-performing executive in one organization can transfer to another job and be almost ineffective. But the reason why it is so problematic is because it is assumed that social influence only goes in one direction: from the executive to the company. In reality, though, it is much more of a two-way inter-action. If someone finds themselves working in a context with different assumptions about the working world, different cultural practices, and different styles of personal interaction, it is unlikely that they will be able to exert the same type of influence unless they change their own working habits. We may have preferred or consistent styles, but the manner in which those styles find expres-sion can be very different.

Belbin's typology is undoubtedly valuable in showing how people can make different contributions to a team's work, and how positive team action often requires a mixture of different types of activity. However, it is better to think of team roles as just that – types of activity – and it may not be all that helpful to think of individual people as automatically representing the appro-priate roles.

Team skills

An alternative to the team role approach is to look at teams in terms of the skills which the members bring to them. Katzenbach and Smith (1993) emphasize the importance of ensuring that a team has the appropriate balance of skills needed to undertake that particular job. These skills fall into three groups. The first group is that set of skills involving technical or functional **expertise**. Any task which requires the setting up of a team to undertake it is likely to need certain kinds of expert knowledge. That may involve knowledge of more than one kind: for example, an attempt to develop computer-aided note-taking systems for doctors wouldn't be likely to succeed if it only involved computer experts, since it would also require expert knowledge of the demands of the doctor's job. So the team would have to ensure that it included both types of expertise.

The second type of skill needed by a team is to do with **problem-solving** and decision-making. It is one thing knowing that there is a problem to be solved; but the team also needs to be able to identify the nature of the problem, evaluate options and interventions, make decisions about what would be the most effective way to take action and how they should go about it. In a working team, people will often develop these skills as they tackle the problem, but it can be useful if some of the team members have some of these skills beforehand.

The third type of skill is to do with the way that **interpersonal interaction** takes place in the group. A team isn't likely to function well unless its members are able to communicate effectively with one another and unless it is able to get over the interpersonal problems and conflicts which can often arise between individuals. Again, these skills are often acquired as the team members come to know one another and as it proceeds with its task; it is often useful, however, to have at least some members of the team who are interpersonally skilled enough to see conflict coming and head it off.

This approach to effective teamwork contains a number of very different assumptions from that put forward by Belbin. One of those assumptions is the idea of development over time: since the people who make up the team are human beings, they will learn, adapt and adjust their ways of working as they gain in experience. Belbin's model, by contrast, sees people in a far more static manner. It's like a jigsaw puzzle: assemble the right components, slot them together and the picture will emerge. The fact that the people themselves may change – and often do – isn't really taken into account.

The group and the team

So let's get back to the original question of this chapter: what's the difference between a working group, and a team? Perhaps the most important difference can be summed up in one sentence: a team is a group of people actively co-operating to achieve the same goal or purpose. Team members work **with** one another to achieve their goals: they don't just get on with their own jobs and leave other people to get on with theirs. At the same time, they co-operate – they don't try to interfere with other people, or make it difficult for them to work efficiently. Instead, they direct their activities towards helping the other team members, too, to work towards the team's goal. According to Adair (1986) this is the key difference between the team and the group: the contributions of individuals in a team are complementary to one another, whereas in a group the members are largely interchangeable.

Teams and organizational status

Another big difference between a working group and a team has to do with status. A working group, to be effective, needs to be composed of people who have the same, or nearly the same, status within the organization. Having a 'boss' present, or someone of very different status indeed, often inhibits the sense of cohesion in the group – people feel less close to one another and are less inclined to communicate freely. But in a team, differences of status don't matter, because each individual's contribution is respected since it helps to get the job done.

So a functioning team will often welcome people of higher status, because they will help the team to operate more effectively. A team member who has the authority to make decisions, or to speak directly with those who can, isn't seen as an 'outsider', but as someone who will help the team to get on with their job. Their status is an asset, rather than a hindrance to communication. Effectively, in social identity terms, they become seen as 'one of us' rather than 'one of them'. And that makes all the difference.

We don't need to think that we are the same as everyone else in order to feel that we 'belong' in the team. Indeed, social identity theory tells us that we can accept a lot of individual differences in our special team or 'in-group' – as long as everyone subscribes to the fundamental values and assumptions. As we saw earlier, José Marques and his colleagues showed that we will tolerate very deviant behaviour from 'in-group members', while the same behaviour from someone who is an 'outsider' can be regarded with severe disapproval. Rather than insisting that everyone should be the same, good working teams often take pride in the very different abilities of their members.

Japanese managers have known this for many years, of course. Many Japanese industries are organized in terms of working teams, with members of different status and skills. These teams make sure that the part of the work that they are responsible for is carried out as well as possible – and they take that task very seriously. Any idea which might improve the job, even a little bit, is investigated seriously and implemented if it seems to work – something which the team can do, because it has the necessary authority among the team's members. They don't have to wait for the idea to pass upwards through layers of management and for a decision eventually to come down from 'on high' to tell them to go ahead.

Usually, we find that managers of high-performance, team-based organizations, whether Western or Japanese, have little time for the trappings of status which are so common in more conventional organizations – they will wear the same type of clothes, eat in the same canteen and be addressed in the same way as the others working in the company. All this subtly fosters the idea that they and the work-force are all working towards the same goals – that they are all part of the same large-scale team. The result is that information flows more freely around the company and that petty resentments caused by people being insensitive to relative status are minimized. It isn't a requirement of effective team management, of course – but as both management practice and social identity theory show us, it helps a lot when managers and work-force see each other as being on the 'same side'!

SUMMARY

- A team differs from a working group in that it is fundamentally task-oriented and composed of people with different, but complementary, knowledge and skills.
- Research into group norms shows that they exert powerful control over group members, which helps to define the group and keep it functioning smoothly and appropriately. Team norms tend to be more task-focused than the norms of ordinary working groups.
- Group cohesion is an important factor in teamworking and it can be seen as deriving from the human tendency for social identification. Both formal and informal communication play an important part in establishing cohesion. The use of visible signs such as specialized clothing, however, is less likely to be effective.
- Personal constructs are the individual ways that we understand our worlds. They mean that we interpret information so that it makes

sense to us on our own terms. Differences in personal constructs can sometimes produce misunderstandings or failures of communication.

- Research has shifted in emphasis from group roles to team roles, reflecting a more task-focused approach. However, a weakness of the role approach is that it assumes that people will fall into 'types' and ignores the transactional and interactional dimensions of people's behaviour.
- Team skills tend to fall into three groups: those relating to technical or functional expertise, those to do with effective problem-solving and those to do with interpersonal interaction and social harmony.
- Rigid organizational status distinctions can present a serious barrier to effective team working and organizations which have adopted a team-working approach often act to minimize the trappings and signals of status.

Box 2.4 **Management recommendations**

Take a close look at the norms and values which appear to be operating in your department or company. Distinguish the pivotal norms from the peripheral ones and examine them carefully. If they need changing, open up discussions with the staff as to how that might be achieved.

Explore the communication factors operating on the team: general factors relating to the organization and the team's role in it; specific factors to do with the team's task.

Provide opportunities for informal communication, such as social events or out-of-the-ordinary training experiences. These will also encourage group cohesion.

Examine the status distinctions in your organization with a critical eye and do away with as many of them as possible.

3 Building a team

A team, as we've seen, is a group of people who work together to achieve a common goal. This might mean the carrying out of a particular task, or the establishment of a smooth-running function (a management team, for instance, has many different tasks to carry out, but it generally has a common goal). At the risk of sounding obvious, this implies that building a team means ensuring that the members of the team really do have common goals and that they can work together to achieve them.

Common goals can't just be taken for granted. For example, some members of a management team might see their goal as the maintenance of effective working systems and practices within the organization, while others might see it as retaining and increasing the overall market share, or others might consider it to be the maintenance of a desirable stock market image. Ideally, of course, all three of these would fit together automatically; but in the rather more patchy real world, such a diversity of goals can lead to very different assumptions and working practices, which need to be sorted out before the management is able to act fully as a team.

SOME PRINCIPLES OF TEAM-BUILDING

There are many ways of building a team and almost all of them, indirectly, draw on certain basic mechanisms in human nature. The traditional military manner of building a team, for instance, involved putting a group of people through all sorts of shared and demanding experiences. Being cold, hungry, exhausted and having to struggle simply to survive establishes a common understanding between the people who are sharing the experience. This is reinforced if actually managing to get through the experience demands co-operation and teamwork. Military systems have traditionally managed to create teams out of collections of individuals through establishing the bond of common experience in this way. A similar process (although possibly less extreme) happened in many public schools, of course, forming the 'old boy network' so apparent in the higher levels of government and management in Britain.

Although some approaches to team-building have involved similar types of experiences, usually based around outdoor activities and residential weekends, others have taken a somewhat gentler approach. Even though team builders still aim to ensure that the members of the team get to know one another very well, they generally take the view that this can be achieved in rather less drastic manner.

The main priority

Above all else, building a team involves developing a strong and positive sense of 'belonging'. Unless the team members can identify with óne another – can see their team as 'us' rather than just a collection of individuals – a team can't possibly work. The reason for this lies deep in human nature: we are social animals, and we evolved in close-knit groups of families and tribes. We feel most secure when we are co-operating with others and when we are with people that we feel to be friends and allies. And we work best and most inventively, when we feel secure. It's obvious really: after all, it's bound to be a strain looking over your shoulder for enemies or competitors all the time. It drains your energies, and those energies can be channelled much more profitably into work.

So the task of building a team involves creating conditions in which people will begin to perceive the team members as 'us' – as belonging to the same unit and identifying with it. This excludes 'outsiders', of course, but that doesn't mean that it is about 'goodies' and 'baddies'. People can maintain many different social identities and different groups can co-operate easily. It is only when there is a perceived competition for resources that co-operation breaks down. But if the team members don't see themselves as 'us' – if they look to other groups for their social identification – then the team is a team in name only. Really, it's just a collection of individuals.

The organizational context

One of the most important aspects of team-building, and one which is often badly overlooked, is the wider context in which the team can operate. Managers who are implementing teamworking for the first time often fail to appreciate how obstructive traditional organizational structures can be. For example, it is relatively easy to set up teams whose role is to come up with proposals as to how the work could be made more effective. But all too often, such proposals face obstruction from higher levels in the hierarchy who see them as unnecessary (often without being aware of the realistic working conditions). New proposals become lost without trace, or experience lengthy and demoralizing delays so that by the time they are implemented, they are hardly worthwhile. In such situations, it is hardly surprising that the team becomes much less enthusiastic about making proposals at all, until eventually it is thoroughly demotivated.

There can be other ways that the wider organization will subtly undermine teamworking, too. For example, a personnel department may insist on individual appraisal and reward systems which take no notice of a team's achievements and which fail to acknowledge the importance of shared effort. Or the organization may insist on team members with different skills, drawn from different departments, remaining within their previous line management structure. This will inevitably make an imbalance in the amount that team members can contribute to the team, as well as making it difficult for the team's manager to make necessary decisions about deployment, training and new opportunities.

For this reason, effective teamworking also requires support at high levels within the organization: it isn't something which can be implemented independently at the lower levels. A team needs to know who it can turn to for advice and support; who in the organization will be prepared to make it easier for the team to function and how it can deal with the traditional patterns of authority yet still respond to the challenges and demands of its own task. We will be dealing with these issues in more detail in Chapter 6, but they need to be mentioned here because it would be

Box 3.1   **Learned helplessness**

The effects of bad management styles don't just vanish when a new management takes over. In large organizations, the **learned helplessness** generated by obstructive or excessively authoritarian systems can persist for years, preventing people in those organizations from taking action, or from responding to change initiatives.

Learned helplessness is a passive condition which develops in both human beings and animals, when they find themselves in an unpleasant situation where nothing they can do can make it any better. At first, both people and animals do what they can to change an unpleasant situation, or escape from it. But if all of the possibilities are blocked, they become passive and stop making any efforts at all. That's understandable. But what is more important is that they remain passive even when the situation has changed and they could quite easily improve things simply by trying a previous activity again, or doing something different.

This is graphically illustrated in the case of an academic department in a middle-sized university. For one reason or another, this department had experienced negative and demoralizing management for many years. Initiatives suggested by the staff were blocked by the administrative hierarchy, research contracts were obstructed and lost because of unwieldy organizational decision-making, and attempts to set up conferences or training days were made so difficult by a turgid bureaucracy that nobody ever made more than one attempt. The department's leaders were not politically sophisticated and, as a result, political manoeverings from other sectors of the university meant that it had been systematically under-funded and under-resourced.

As might be expected, the departmental staff responded by developing an inward-looking, 'us against the world' focus. They concentrated on their own work, resisted change as much as possible and regarded the higher administrative structures of the university with deep suspicion.

Eventually, however, the senior management of the university changed and more open, less political systems, began to develop. A new head of faculty was also appointed, who adopted a shrewd and dynamic way of liaising with upper management. These developments opened up new avenues for the department concerned who, since they were very popular with students and received a high number of applications, were in a strong position in the new market-conscious environment.

The department was officially encouraged to expand, as higher management began to recognize its strengths. Had they been prepared to use their new position to bargain with the university hierarchy, they could have made significant improvements to their teaching resources and staffing allocations. Indeed, this had already happened in a very similar department belonging to a different university, which had embraced the market changes and ensured that they worked to the department's benefit. But in this case, the longer-standing staff had become so accustomed to the idea that they were a victimized group, that they felt there was no point in making any attempt to do anything. It was a classic case of learned helplessness.

The department continued to resist change as much as it could and the staff rehearsed their grievances frequently to one another, while resenting and resisting every increase in their student numbers. They made no attempt to take advantage of their new situation, but insisted that nothing was really any different. Eventually, of course, the positive orientation from higher management began to disappear. The department's learned helplessness had prevented them from capitalizing on an opportunity which could have benefited them a great deal.

unrealistic to give the impression that building a team is simply a matter of training the team's members. As Box 3.1 shows, learned helplessness can be a very real factor in organizations and it is one which can be generated very quickly in a team which is trying to operate in a continually obstructive organizational context.

FOUR DIFFERENT APPROACHES

When we look at the various approaches to team-building which are described in the organizational literature it is possible to distinguish four general approaches, within which the various techniques can be classified. I have named these the interpersonal approach, the role-definition approach, the values approach, and the task-based approach. Each of them has some useful characteristics and each has demonstrated its effectiveness at different times – although some may be more suited to the modern working environment than others. I shall begin by giving a brief overview of the four approaches before discussing the principles underlying each one in more detail.

The first approach – the **interpersonal** approach – focuses on developing very high levels of social and personal awareness between team members, for example, by helping team members to learn how to listen to one another, or to become aware of the past experiences of the other members of the team. The idea is that a better understanding of one another's personalities, and a better ability to communicate with one another, will help people to work together more easily. It will encourage people to to see the other team members as 'us', rather than simply as a collection of people that they have to work with.

A second approach to team-building focuses on the **roles and norms** which exist within the team. In Chapter 2, we saw how Benne and Sheats, Belbin and others developed typologies of team roles, which defined the different types of intervention which people could make when they were participating in a team. For some management consultants, this way of understanding teams became the framework which defined how a team could be built, and so team-building emphasised role definition as a major task. The aim was to clarify each individual's role expectations, the norms of the group as a whole and the shared responsibilities of the different group members. This would mean that the team would become aware of itself as a working unit. It would be able to operate effectively and efficiently because each member had a clear understanding of their place, role and responsibility (e.g. Bennis 1966).

A third approach to team-building also focuses on developing a shared understanding between team members. This time, though, the emphasis is on the overall stance which the team members take towards what they are doing and the **values** which they adopt, rather than the characters of the individuals making up the team or the roles which they are playing. For example, West (1994) proposed a model of team-building in which the most important factor was that the team should develop a clear shared understanding of its values and aims. In this model one of the most fundamental features of team management is the development of explicit 'mission statements', negotiated and shared by all who are expected to participate in the team. By ensuring that everyone in the team holds common values and that the working aims of the team actually reflect those values, it is felt that the team members will be able to work together effectively, and will be able to perceive how their own personal activity contributes to the team's shared aims and reflects its shared values.

A fourth approach to team-building emphasizes the **team's task** and the unique way that each team member can contribute to the achievement of that task. In this approach, the emphasis is not so much on what people are like, as on what skills they have and how those skills can contribute to the whole. This approach, therefore, places a heavy emphasis on the interchange of information between the various team members. It also emphasizes the realistic analysis of the team's task in terms of the resources, skills and practical steps which it will require to carry its task out. This approach is manifest in many current discussions of high-performance teamworking (e.g. Katzenbach and Smith 1993).

Most, if not all, methods of team-building derive from one of these four approaches. Their effectiveness depends on three factors: the context in which the team is being built; the nature of the people involved; and the types of organizational task which the team is expected to carry out. But what all of these approaches have in common, of course, is that they tap into the very deep psychological mechanisms of **social identification**. We will be looking at the social identity approach to team-building later in this chapter, but for now we will explore some of the ideas and principles of the four main approaches in a little more detail.

The interpersonal approach to team-building

The interpersonal approach, as we have just seen, emphasizes the interpersonal nature of team work; and takes the implicit view that, if people understand one another well enough, they will work together effectively. It has its roots in the humanistic psychology which emerged in the 1950s as a reaction to the mechanistic psychology of the behaviourists. In organizational work, it has taken many different forms, with different degrees of structure. But in essence, the principle is that open and candid discussions of relationships, conflicts and 'hidden agendas' within the group will generate an atmosphere of mutual trust and confidence and so build effective teamworking.

Carl Rogers, t-groups and sensitivity training

One of the most influential practitioners and theoreticians in the humanistic school was Carl Rogers, known as the 'father' of counselling. Rogers took the view that human beings had two very fundamental, but often unconscious, psychological needs, both of which had to be satisfied. The first of these is a need for **positive regard** (love, affection or – probably more important in organizational terms – respect) from other people. The second is a need for **self-actualization**: a need to develop and make real (actualize) one's own abilities and potential. If the first need wasn't satisfied, Rogers argued, then the person would spend their time approval-seeking, and this would interfere with their tendency to self-actualize. But in working terms, the tendency to self-actualize is the most valuable, since it is this tendency which will motivate people to rise to challenges, to develop their own skills to the best of their ability and to learn new ones.

Rogers believed very firmly that all that was needed to allow the self-actualizing tendency to come to the fore was a climate of unconditional positive regard. By that, he meant positive regard (approval, liking etc) for the individual as a person, which didn't depend on that person acting in an approved way. That didn't mean that everything had to be accepted – in Rogers' terms, it was quite OK to disapprove of something that the individual had done, but not to transfer that disapproval to the person themselves. Unconditional positive regard would result in the person feeling emotionally safe and with that need satisfied, they would be able to contribute more fully to their organization.

Rogers' work led to the development of a number of team-building approaches which emphasized developing close interpersonal relationships and a high degree of positive regard and affection. The most common of these, which was very popular in the 1960s although it actually dated from the 1940s, was the **t-group**. People joining a team group engaged in a variety of sensitivity training and other exercises designed to bring them emotionally closer to the other members of the group and to help them to work through personal inhibitions and traumas which prevented them from interacting openly with other people. T-groups were generally residential, lasting from two to four days, and took place away from the working context. Those who participated in them were ideally not known to each other previously, since it was felt that would encourage reluctance and inhibit openness; but the principle was that the experience would 'cleanse' the individual, giving them more self-understanding and freeing them to act openly and positively with their colleagues when they returned to work.

The openness movement also left its mark on team-building strategies. Less extreme, more directive encounter groups used techniques derived from Rogerian principles, aiming to develop interpersonal skills between people who were already working as a team. Typically, all members of the team would go away on a residential weekend or day out and engage in exercises designed to increase their interpersonal sensitivity: listening skills training, trust-building exercises, alertness and noticing exercises and so on. Each of these exercises would help the team members to become more aware of each other and how they were likely to react in different situations. They also produced a common shared experience, and helped to create that sense of 'us' which is so important in a working team. In the organizational contexts of the 1960s and 1970s, which meant that people were receptive to this type of approach, these approaches to team-building were often very successful.

Although they were a popular management training exercise at the time, the openness approach gradually fell from favour. Kaplan (1986) discussed the way that by the mid-1980s, things had reached the point where anything resembling a T-group or encounter group had become *verboten* in many organizations. Kaplan attributed this decline to a number of excesses and abuses in the openness movement, which had sometimes resulted in a lack of recognition of the organization's needs or of its practical constraints. The lessening of interest in the openness approach was mirrored in other fields, too: Figure 3.1 illustrates the decline of published references to t-groups and encounter-groups in organizational, clinical and educational contexts, during the twenty-year period from 1974–1994.

Transactional analysis

Another, more structured, example of the interpersonal approach was developed by Eric Berne, who devoted much of his time to looking at how people interact with one another in everyday life. This approach emphasizes the kind of transactions which take place between people – so it is known as **transactional analysis**. Although Berne's model has sometimes been criticized as a bit simplistic, it has proved itself to be very useful in a great many organizational settings, because it helps us to understand how many seemingly irrational – but very common – problems arise

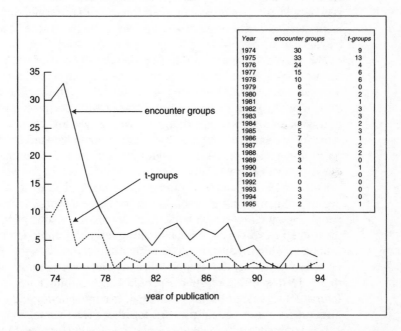

Year	encounter groups	t-groups
1974	30	9
1975	33	13
1976	24	4
1977	15	6
1978	10	6
1979	6	0
1980	6	2
1981	7	1
1982	4	3
1983	7	3
1984	8	2
1985	5	3
1986	7	1
1987	6	2
1988	8	2
1989	3	0
1990	4	1
1991	1	0
1992	0	0
1993	3	0
1994	3	0
1995	2	1

Figure 3.1 Database references to t-groups and encounter groups from 1974 to 1995

(*source*: Psyclit Research Abstract Database)

between people working together and particularly between managers and employees.

Berne proposed that, when we are dealing with one another, we can do so in one of three possible ego-states. In the Adult ego-state, we act as mature, sensible human beings – we communicate with one another easily, we don't let emotional distortions produce quarrels or resentments and we are ready to take responsibility for our own actions. This state, Berne argues, is when we work best: we are able to function well and efficiently in an Adult ego-state.

A second ego-state which Berne identified, and which it is very easy for people to slip into, is that of the Parent. In the parental ego-state, we become overly affected by our own responsibilities and this affects how we interact with other people. In particular, it affects how we interact with our subordinates. We give orders, we insist that everyone respects our position and authority – and shows it – and we don't take other people's points of view into account. The Parent ego-state, therefore, is authoritarian, dictatorial and even at its best, distinctly patronizing towards subordinates.

The third ego-state which Berne identified is that of the Child. In the Child ego-state, we become dependent, emotional and approval-seeking. As a result, we don't take initiatives and are unwilling to accept responsibility for what we do. We prefer to be told what to do, so that if things go wrong, we can blame others rather than ourselves. We also expect the people who are in higher positions to see to the things which we are concerned about and feel aggrieved if they don't.

These three ego-states, as you might imagine, can exert a great deal of influence on the nature of interactions at work. When two people are interacting with one another in the Adult ego-state, they do so as responsible adults, taking a mature approach to the problems which they are encountering and trying to solve those problems intelligently. But very easily, and particularly where there are disparities of status, people can slip into Parent/Child interactions, which become emotional, irrational and make it very difficult for those people to work together effectively.

For teamwork, this makes a great deal of difference. A team can't function if some of its members are overly ready to become resentful and emotional because they feel overlooked. Nor can it

Box 3.2   **Parent-child ego-states**

Some forms of management encourage parent-child ego states without realizing it. An accountancy firm (which we will call 'Counters') had, like many other small companies, been founded by a small group of technically competent individuals who had decided to group together to form a small company of their own. As they had opened up new areas of work, they had taken on more employees and, at the point of my consultancy visit, were employing about 20 staff. However, they had a massively high rate of staff turnover, which was why they wanted the consultancy.

When I arrived, I was somewhat dismayed to find that the desks of the staff were arranged in rows, with a senior member of staff working at a desk in front of, and facing, the others. The effect was exactly like a school, with the 'teacher' at the front supervising the 'class'. In fact, the arrangement was also symptomatic of the way that those directors regarded their employees – rather than regarding them as competent, professional individuals, they were constantly prepared for the staff to cause 'trouble' and did not trust any of them with responsibility or even very minor decision-making.

The desk arrangement had been entirely unconscious, yet what it had actually done was to convey a message to the employees that they were to be watched and controlled. In transactional analysis terms, the relationships between employees and director were in Child and Parent mode: the employees were treated like children, while the founder-directors acted the part of parents – some more strictly than others, but all unconsciously taking on that idea of their role. Naturally enough, this produced Child-style behaviour from the employees: there was a great deal of grumbling and discontentment, an unwillingness to put in any extra effort, resentment of the directors' cavalier attitude and very low work motivation. But nobody challenged the directors directly.

On my second visit to Counters, after this and several other issues had been discussed with the directors, there was a very different atmosphere. Once they had become aware of these issues, the founder-directors were able to do something about them and had tried to do so. The most visible outcome was the desks, which were arranged in small groups, making it easier for staff engaged in the same project to discuss their work with one another (conversation had previously been discouraged as a 'distraction'). Other company policies had been put in place designed to give employees more feedback and to encourage them to take more responsibility for minor parts of their work.

As a result, the employees acted more professionally, enjoyed their work more and were working harder. In transactional analysis terms, the directors and employees had moved towards Adult/Adult transactions rather than Parent/ Child ones. The outcome was a more professional company, with much less discontent and a lower rate of staff turnover.

function if its members are dictatorial and dominating with one another. But people are often entirely unaware of these ego-states and can slip into them very easily. So transactional analysis training helps people to become aware of this type of interaction and this can often be very positive in building a team.

The various types of interpersonal approach are not mutually exclusive, of course. Many facilitators (the openness school of thought deliberately avoided the term 'leaders' in order to emphasize the fact that everyone in the group contributed) use transactional analysis as well as sensitivity training exercises to good effect. Indeed, the combination of the two has survived to this day and is still effective in building some types of team, although it is usually adopted in public-and voluntary-sector organizational contexts rather than in commercial ones.

The role-definition approach

Team-building activities based on the role-definition approach, as one might expect, tend to put a strong emphasis on clarifying the roles and role expectations of group members. In its early days, this often involved very direct interpersonal discussion. For example, the role negotiation approach developed by Harrison (1972a) involved each team member making a straightforward appraisal of their working situation and then identifying things which other people could do which would help to increase their personal effectiveness.

Each team member would list what they felt they needed from each of the other team members, using three categories: things that the other person should do more of, or do better; things that they should do less of, or stop doing; and things that they should carry on doing. Then the team members would get together in pairs to discuss their lists and to negotiate contracts between each other – 'if you will do this, then I will do that'. The contracts would be written down and signed by both parties, with an understanding that if one person failed to keep to their side of the bargain, then the other person was free to withdraw from theirs.

This approach to team-building is very different from the interpersonal one, even though it still has honesty and candour as its basis. The main difference lies in its focus of attention: people's individual feelings, beliefs and hidden conflicts are seen as totally irrelevant, and what is important is what people do and what they need from others. According to this model, as long as people are open about what they require from the other person in terms of work, then that is enough. There is no need for more in-depth personal analysis.

Later, team-building based on this approach tended to use rather more sophisticated models like the one put forward by Benne and Sheats (see Table 2.2 in Chapter 2). This, as we saw in Chapter 2, articulated group task roles, group building and maintenance roles and self-centred roles. Team-building exercises were then developed, which would engage the team members in various tasks, which allowed the various types of role to come to the fore. The type of task used in team-building according to this model might be anything from a discussion of a controversial topic to a complex model-building exercise.

The team members would be observed while they took part in the task and their behaviour and actions would be classified by the observers in terms of the type of role which they were perceived to be adopting. When the exercise, or set of exercises, was over, the observations were 'reflected' back to the participants – in other words, the team members were told how they had acted and how their behaviour fitted into the role categories. The idea was that feedback about their own actions would allow team members to see their actions 'from a distance' and more constructively. This would help them to become aware of habitual or destructive roles, and perhaps take on more constructive ones.

This general strategy for team-building using the role-definition approach has remained reasonably consistent over time, although the models and typologies which team-building consultants have adopted do vary. For example, in 1950, Bales developed a typology of the different interpersonal processes which go on within groups, which was designed to allow trainers and other people to focus on how interaction occurs. This led to team-building exercises which focused on the interpersonal processes which were occurring during teamwork – and particularly in group decision-making – rather than on the specific roles team members were adopting.

The categories which are used for Bales' interaction process analysis are listed in Table 3.1. As you can see from the table, they emphasize verbal interactions, of the sort that happen in team and other meetings and this reflects the model's orientation towards decision-making, advice or involvement teams rather than action or production teams (see Chapter 1). The eight categories delineate different types of activity, of the sort likely to be found in committees or project discussions, ranging from giving support to asking for opinions and suggestions, or showing disagreement.

Team-building based on Bales' interpersonal process model usually involves training the people concerned to understand the various interpersonal processes and how they work. Team members are introduced to the categories and sometimes given a little practice in using them to code videos of meetings. Then they observe a meeting of the rest of their own team. While observing, they concentrate on taking note of the interpersonal processes which are occurring, rather than following the content of the meeting. The person who has been observing then feeds their observations back to the group and they all discuss what these observations reveal.

The value of using the categories in this way is that they reveal when a team is only using a limited range of interaction processes. For instance, the members of a particular team may give opinions a great deal, but rarely ask other team members for theirs.

Table 3.1   Categories for interaction process analysis (adapted from Bales 1950)

Category	Examples
Gives support	Helping, rewarding, building on suggestions, raising others' esteem, showing acceptance.
Gives suggestion	Making proposals, suggesting direction, offering opportunity for others to contribute.
Gives opinion	Evaluating or analysing ideas, expressing feelings or wishes, interpreting, imposing own ideas.
Gives information	Contributing new facts, repeating or rephrasing previous contributions, clarifying, confirming.
Asks for information	Seeking facts or information, asking for reiteration or clarification.
Asks for opinion	Seeking feelings or wishes, asking for interpretations or evaluations from others.
Asks for suggestions	Seeking ideas, directions or proposals, looking for ways of taking action.
Shows disagreement	Showing resistance or rejection, withholding help, defending, antagonizing others, attacking others.

Alternatively, the team may discover that in a typical discussion, nobody at all gives support for ideas which are put forward. Sometimes, of course, it is an external consultant who does the observation and the reflecting, but the usual view is that the method is more effective when team members themselves are directly involved.

The role of the consultant in team-building exercises of this sort does matter, though, since learning to distance oneself from the content of a discussion and focus on the interpersonal processes is a tricky task, which needs training and guidance. It is also the consultant's role to help the team to discuss what their findings mean and show how they may be used to guide the team into more effective operation.

Some team-building interventions of this sort take the set of team roles developed by Belbin (1981) as their starting point rather than the Bales interpersonal process categories. These roles

Table 3.2   Principles of team-building (adapted from Belbin 1981)

1. Each team member contributes both a function and a team role.
2. A team needs an optimal balance between functional and team roles, depending on its task.
3. Team effectiveness depends on how far team members identify and adjust to relative strengths within the team.
4. Some team members fit some team roles better than others, depending on their personality and mental abilities.
5. A team can only deploy its technical resources to the best advantages when it has a suitable range and balance of team roles.

were listed in Table 2.3, and as we saw in the last chapter, tend to be more task-oriented than earlier models. Belbin had developed his model through analysing successful and unsuccessful teams, and concluded that there were five principles for building an effective team. These principles are listed in Table 3.2. Another model which has proved popular with team-building consultants is the 'Team management wheel' developed by Margerison McCann, and illustrated in Figure 2.1 (Chapter 2).

Another variant of this approach is the use of highly active adventure-training days or weekends. The team members are removed from their day to day environment to engage in strenuous physical activities, such as mountain-climbing, canoeing, or developing survival skills. These activities are designed to bring out leadership as well as team skills, and have been a very popular form of management training, although an empirical study of their effectiveness reported by Ibbetson and Newell (1995) found rather equivocal results.

Although the precise model used can vary, the essential principles of team-building in this approach remain very similar. The main value of the role-definition approach lies in the way that it allows team members to see themselves 'from the outside', as it were. This lets team members reflect on their own styles of interaction, and teaches them how to adjust their personal style in ways which will help the team as a whole to operate more effectively.

The values approach

For West (1994), as we saw earlier, the focus of team-building is on developing a consensus between the members of the team about the shared values and principles which they are applying to their work. Indeed, sharing a common vision of the work is regarded in this model as being the defining characteristic of a team – without that, it is simply a group of individuals. It is only having a common purpose which holds people together, makes them feel able to work co-operatively with one another, and allows a sense of 'them and us' to develop.

According to this model, therefore, one of the primary tasks in developing an effective team is to establish that consensus of vision. Team-building begins with discussion, debate and exploration of ideas, as people begin to articulate what they feel is important about the work which they are doing and about the way that the team itself should operate. To begin in this way is important, West argues, because it minimizes later problems or conflicts arising from incompatible goals on the part of team members. And developing a shared vision is something which needs to be done with a great deal of care. West identified five dimensions of team vision, which are listed in Table 3.3.

This type of team-building is particularly valuable in situations where the team's work is continuous rather than the completion of a particular task and involves a high level of independent decision-making. Long-term teams of this kind need to have a very high level of mutual understanding, since there is such a high potential for conflicting advice or actions between different members of the team. It is also particularly useful when the team members come from many different professions. For example, a child care team might include a social worker, a district nurse, a residential case officer, a paediatrician, an educational psychologist and several others. Each of these will bring different ideas and professional assumptions to the team's work, and the team will require a great deal of debate and discussion before it is able to develop a fully shared and fully articulated set of team values.

Teams of this kind can often consist of individuals belonging to different organizations. However, the emphasis on the underlying shared values and vision of the team also reflects the increasing recognition of the importance of shared values in organizational life. Increasingly, organizational researchers have come to recognize the importance of having a set of common beliefs or assumptions which can guide the way that we approach our own work, as well as our interactions with other people. In Chapters 6 and 7 we

Table 3.3 Dimensions of team vision (adapted from West 1994)

Clarity	The goals, values and orientations of the team have to be clearly established and doing this can sometimes take a great deal of discussion.
Motivating value	The vision must be something which the team members belive in and are prepared to work to achieve.
Attainability	The team vision must be something which the team can actually manage – there's no point setting unrealistic or unattainable goals, because that just makes people more inclined to give up.
Sharedness	It is vital that all team members share the vision, because otherwise they are likely to find themselves working at cross-purposes, or unable to reconcile basic conflicts.
Future potential	The vision must contain an ability to develop further in the future. There's no point having a team vision which is fixed and unalterable, because people change, organizations change, and the nature of the work changes. The team's vision needs to be reviewed regularly to make sure that it is still appropriate for new situations and circumstances.

will be looking at how these ideas connect with research into organizational culture and how the team and the organization can work effectively together.

Maintaining the team

Building a team is one thing: ensuring that it stays a team and doesn't become either ineffective or fragmented, is quite another. West (1994) emphasizes the importance of building in regular, systematic mechanisms to evaluate the team's work. These can be used for evaluating the contributions of individual team members, for monitoring the team's performance as a whole and for making sure that there is frequent communication and review of progress within the team. In other words, by incorporating regular mechanisms for team review and appraisal, it is possible to give feedback both to individuals and to the team as a whole. It also helps to establish the sense of mutual interaction and common action which is necessary if social identification with the team is to be maintained.

West (1994) suggests that it is particularly valuable for the whole team to take time out: to engage in team-building on an away-day where people are able to appraise themselves and their actions in a different context. The new situation allows people to look at what they are doing more clearly, without becoming bogged down in details and so it helps team members to focus once again on their shared vision. In this way, the team members can see how their own recent actions fit with the shared purpose and vision of the team, they can develop new ideas and they can explore new possibilities with one another. 'Away-day' sessions, West argues, can also be used to give a team a new lease of life if it seems to be becoming tired or jaded – and even if the team is functioning well, they can be a useful 'refresher'.

The task-oriented approach

The task-oriented approach to team-building, as we have seen, emphasizes the task which the team actually has to perform. In this approach, teams are made aware of the challenges which that task offers and encouraged to explore the implications of those challenges explicitly. Typically, they are given learning experiences which allow them to identify and refine the particular skills which the task will require, and they are encouraged to set specific goals which will allow them to identify their progress towards achievement of the team's task.

In this approach, the organizational task which the team is expected to perform is taken as paramount – and it is assumed that all team members share that assumption. Personal feelings, 'hidden agendas' and the like are not considered to be a valid part of the team's activity: achieving the working target is the only thing which is important. So team-building activities, too, emphasize specific tasks which will help the team to reach their goals: defining timetables and sub-tasks, training decision-making skills, and developing strategies to overcome obstacles.

This approach is particularly well reflected in high-performance teams, such as those described by Katzenbach and Smith (1993). These teams are quite different from, say, those described by West (1994). West's research largely concerns long-term teams with ongoing, never-completed tasks like patient care, but Katzenbach's research concerns high-powered executive teams, brought together in equally high-powered organizations to carry out a

Table 3.4   Building task-focused teams (source: Katzenbach and Smith 1993)

1. Establish urgency and direction
2. Select team members based on skills and skill potential, not personalities
3. Pay particular attention to first meetings and actions
4. Set some clear rules of behaviour
5. Set and seize upon a few immediate performance-oriented tasks and goals
6. Challenge the group regularly with fresh facts and information
7. Spend lots of time together
8. Exploit the power of positive feedback, recognition and reward

single complex task, such as a restructuring of working practices in order to meet a particular challenge. Like West's research teams, executive teams comprise individuals with complementary skills and powers; but unlike West's, they have a very clearly prescribed task to complete and once that has been achieved, the team will be disbanded.

It is largely because of this that high-powered executive teams are able to assume that all members of the team share the same values and so avoid making that the prime team-building activity. Indeed, as far as work is concerned, they do share similar values, since survival at top levels in the kind of high-powered organization described by Katzenbach and Smith is entirely dependent on delivering results. It is quite different from the disparate professional experiences and assumptions apparent in a primary health care team. High-powered executive teams are often intolerant of activities which they see as time-wasting and respond best to team-building activities which they can see are likely to help them to perform efficiently.

Katzenbach and Smith identified a set of eight basic principles for effective team-building in real-life organizational environments. These are listed in Table 3.4. The main value of explicit team-building strategies, in this model, is that these approaches can bring communication or interaction difficulties to the surface, which might otherwise interfere with developing a clear understanding of how the team members operate. In other words, team-building activities act as diagnostic tools to help the team as a whole to function well.

The goal-setting approach

The specific team-building tasks which emphasize this approach tend to fall into two groups. One approach, perhaps most clearly articulated by Locke, Shaw, Saari and Latham (1982) involves making sure that the team is very clear about what they are doing and how far they are along the road to achieving it. This approach emphasizes **goal-setting**, with the overall task being divided into both long-term and short-term goals. Working together, the team develops a clear timetable, which states when each of the sub-goals should be achieved; and these are often combined with structured forms of feedback and assessments of performance.

Locke *et al.* (1982) reported that this approach has a good track record in many private-sector organizations. It has many positive features – for instance, by providing manageable goals as steps along the way, it helps team members to remain focused on the general task. More importantly, though, it allows them to feel that they are actually getting there: that the team's goals are actually being achieved. The regular appraisal and feedback sessions built into this approach to team-building provide opportunities for positive reinforcement and encouragement of team members, and for explicit recognition of what they have achieved. This is invaluable in encouraging people to identify with the team and feel proud of belonging to their team.

The problem-solving approach

The second type of team-building intervention in this category is all about real-life problem-solving. The team members engage in exercises which are designed to simulate their working experiences and to bring out some of the difficulties which the team is facing. These are used to help the team members to articulate and recognize the problems which they are encountering. From there, they take each problem which has been uncovered one at a time. The team focuses on developing a solution to each problem, and working out how the solution can be implemented given the organizational context and constraints which are acting on the team. Using this approach, then, the team learns how to see its problems as manageable and the team members are encouraged to share their expertise and experience in finding solutions to them (Buller and Bell 1986).

Even though structured experiences can be useful, though, they are not as good as the real thing. It is experience which develops high-performance teams most fully. According to Katzenbach and Smith, each challenge that has been successfully surmounted and each problem that has been overcome, adds to the team's competence and – perhaps more importantly – to its awareness of its capabilities. A high-performance team, in this model, learns to excel as a direct result of undertaking challenging tasks. As they deal with them, they acquire new skills and competences through tackling the problems, obstacles, and learning which are required. Through this experience, the team develops a shared history, an awareness of their own achievements and potential, and, more importantly, a high level of mutual knowledge and understanding. It is these which really weld them together as a team.

USING A MIXTURE OF APPROACHES

As you can see, then, there are several different approaches which have been used for building teams. Since every real-life team is different, and has different constraints on its operation, it isn't really practical to make too many comparisons. Each of these models is 'right', in its own way, and is effective in certain types of situation. But they do focus on different aspects of the phenomenon and they have differing amounts of relevance for different types of teams in different types of contexts. Organizational consultants and organizational development specialists generally use a combination of the different models when they are conducting team-building activities, rather than sticking to just one.

Sundstrom, de Meuse and Futrell (1990) performed a major study which involved comparing 13 different research studies of team-building and looking at how effective each of the strategies had been. The researchers found that most of the research projects had used a mixture of different approaches to team-building. But they also found that the various interventions had mixed success rates, largely because most of them only looked at what was happening within the team and not at the external and organizational context within which the team was operating. And this can be crucial.

What is important, according to Sundstrom, de Meuse and Futrell, is that the approach which is used is actually suited to the context in which the team is operating. We will be examining teams in their organizational context in Chapters 6 and 7, but there are one or two generalizations which it is possible to draw out for the evidence. While all teams need to have clear values, West's approach, which emphasizes debating those values explicitly from the beginning, is particularly suited to the public sector, where team tasks may carry on over years and team members come from many different professional backgrounds. That doesn't mean that it is only suited to the public sector, of course – as West showed, it can also work well in some private organizations too. But it is likely to be strongest in that field.

Katzenbach's approach, on the other hand, seems to be most suited to a high-powered, task-oriented commercial environment, in which a team has been given a definite mission and will be disbanded when it has achieved its task successfully. While it is still important that the team has clear and consistent values, it is possible for the team's values to emerge and be debated during the course of the team's activities; they do not necessarily have to be spelt out from the very beginning. But members of that type of team often share more values in the first place than the multi-disciplinary teams of the public sector.

Different types of team, then, involve different approaches to team-building. And most teams seem to benefit from a combination of different approaches, not just one adopted to the exclusion of everything else. But whatever type of team-building strategy is used, it has one principle in common with all the rest. That principle is the building of social identification. At the end of the day, the team members must be able to work together effectively, and with some degree of confidence and trust in one another. They must be able to see the other people in their team as 'us' and not as 'them'.

The social identity approach to team-building

The social identity approach to team-building draws on each of the four approaches which we have just discussed. It has three main aims: first, to create a strong sense of unity and belonging among the team members, which will motivate them to work together and to co-operate to achieve the team's goals. Second, to create a climate of mutual understanding, so that each member of the team is aware of the contributions of the others, and can see how their very different skills, abilities and tasks contribute to the success of the team as a whole. And third, to bring into focus just how and why people can feel proud of belonging to their particular team, and of its contribution to the work of the company as a whole. These three aims express the psychological mechanisms underlying social identification, so they are fundamental to building strong, firmly cohesive teams.

Creating a sense of unity

Creating a strong sense of unity between the people who make up the team means finding ways that the team can see itself as special. It is basic in human psychology for us to classify each other, and ourselves, into in-groups and out-groups. These groupings can take a number of forms: 'we' may be the technical staff while 'they' are the admin people; or, 'we' may be 'those of us who work over this side of the room', while 'they' are 'that lot who work over there' and so on. But when building a team, we need to make sure that it is the team which matters and not some other type of grouping.

There is evidence, too, that the process of categorizing people – or anything else for that matter – into groups seems to result automatically in exaggerating the similarities of those within the group and exaggerating the difference between the group members and outsiders. In an early study, Tajfel and Wilkes showed that even simple tasks like judging the length of lines were influenced by whether the lines had been classified as A or B. Unlabelled lines were perceived accurately, but lines in the same category were seen as being more similar in length than those in different categories – even when they were really exactly the same.

Our social judgements, too, become exaggerated through classification. Almost any experience of organizational life shows how different departments or working units can exaggerate their differences and ignore what they have in common. The rivalry which results can sometimes be beneficial, by stimulating both departments to high performance. More often, though, it is detrimental, because the departments spend time squabbling with one another or engaging in petty politics rather than getting on with the job. Psychological research shows that whether such rivalry becomes positive or not depends to a large extent on whether the two groups are competing for resources. If they are not in direct competition, then they can have a strong sense of unity and friendly, helpful relationships with other groups. But if they are competing with one another for the same resources – or if they believe they are – then the groups are likely to become quite hostile towards one another (Mummendey and Schreiber 1984).

So an important part of team-building involves ensuring that the team is well-defined and that the team members are able to see their team as distinctive. But it also involves making sure that the team is able to co-operate with others in the organization, so that they can get on with their work effectively instead of having to waste time negotiating with other, hostile departments or teams and playing petty political games. Another part of team-building, therefore, involves defining the team's resources clearly, and making sure that these have not been gained at the expense of some other group.

Establishing good communication

Setting boundaries is only part of establishing a group. People also need to see clearly how they and the other team members fit in with the team as a whole. The team needs to be a cohesive group. But this doesn't really have anything to do with its members being similar to one another. Marques and Yzerbyt (1988) showed that people will often tolerate quite deviant behaviour from a 'black sheep' within the group, while being much less tolerant about some 'outsider'. Also, people working in a team are often proud of their differences and special skills: it is outsiders who may seem to be 'all the same'.

Communication is the single most effective factor in establishing group cohesion. It is vital that each group member has an understanding of the way that others contribute to the whole, if the team is to work well together. Communicating information about the job, information about people's abilities and skills and information about successes and achievements allows everyone to see a clearer picture, and to acknowledge their own and others contributions. And communication needs to operate on higher levels too. People holding different values won't be able to communicate clearly with one another, since each will be making different assumptions about what the other understands and takes for granted. And a team needs to share common values if it is to act effectively. So whatever type of team is involved, it is useful to set up some way that the team can spell out its values and come to a consensus about them.

Box 3.3   **Team-building: a cautionary tale**

If we are to engage in any team-building exercise, we need to be very clear about exactly what it is we are trying to achieve. In particular, it is important that the tendency of people to align themselves into 'them-and-us' groups should be harnessed as a part of the team-building process, since it is such a fundamental part of effective teamworking. If the team-building process does not focus attention on where the social identity boundaries are located, the outcome can be counter-productive and even disastrous.

This was vividly illustrated in a case emanating from a prestigious health service research department. It involved a number of specialists – radiographers, physiotherapists, osteopaths etc. who were working together on a particular project. As time progressed, communication between different people involved in the project deteriorated: there were interpersonal squabbles and factions began to emerge. The team manager attempted to redress the situation and to encourage the teams to work together, but this had very little effect. Finally, the team manager arranged for the parties concerned to be sent on a team-building course, in the hope that this would enable them to work together more effectively.

Unfortunately, the course had the opposite effect. When the group returned, it was apparent that their cohesion and team loyalty had indeed increased. However, where before there had been one disorganized group with a couple of factions, now there were two entirely separate and hostile camps. The training had indeed strengthened the teams, in that each person had learned to interact more effectively with some other people involved with the project – but it had not brought the whole group together. As a result, the individuals concerned had become almost incapable of working co-operatively and the project eventually had to be cancelled.

Robinson and Hayes (1994) discussed a situation with very similar potential, in which physicians and computing specialists were working together in an attempt to develop a usable workstation for busy general practictioners. The project, inevitably, involved a great deal of interaction between the designers – the computing specialists – and the physicians. As it progressed, it became apparent that the two groups were not communicating at all well and that the project was in danger of griding to a halt because of rigid 'them-and-us' confrontations.

At this point, a third group was brought in. This consisted of psychologists, whose role was to mediate communication and encourage the two groups to work together as a team. The introduction of this third party served to defuse the growing polarization of the two professional groups and the psychologists were able to head off confrontations before they happened. As a result, the project was brought back on track and enabled to continue. In this case, the intervention stressed working together, cultivating tolerance and understanding of different professional viewpoints, and reducing the salience of the professional grouping to which the indvidual belonged. By making sure that normal professional differences did not develop into total barriers, the project had been rescued before it had got too late.

(source: Robinson and Hayes 1994)

Communication, as everyone who has worked in a large organization knows, doesn't just happen formally through memos and official bulletins and team-building away-days. It happens informally, through friendships and chat. Which is why activities which bring people together socially are very useful for encouraging cohesion. They can't substitute for official information, of course, but social and informal activities consolidate social bonds, and set up the kind of informal, casual friendships which mean that people can co-operate easily with one another, instead of having to act formally all the time. It's for this reason that the office party or team social outing is so valuable to any organization. By allowing people to show their 'human' sides, they build up a basis of shared experience and (with luck) personal friendship, which is invaluable when something needs to get done.

Building a sense of pride in the team

The third aspect of social identification which is so important in team-building involves establishing a sense of pride in the team, so that team members can feel good about belonging to it. Tajfel and Turner (1979) showed that being able to gain a positive sense of self-esteem from the group to which you belong is vital for social identification. If we can't feel good about belonging to our social group, we will try to distance ourselves from the others ('I'm not like the rest of them') or leave it altogether. So apart from communicating information about abilities and skills, it is also important that the team members regularly appraise their team's successes and achievements; and that the team's manager makes sure that others in the organization also become aware of the team's achievements. In this respect, the social identity approach is closely linked with the task-oriented system proposed by Katzenbach and Smith (1993): the idea is that pride in the team's work and a feeling of identification are most likely to result from knowing that the team has done a good job, and is continuing to do so.

Another way of building team pride is by enhancing the team members' sense of professionalism. Training has a doubly beneficial effect on people at work. One benefit, of course, is that the person gets to learn something from the training itself. But an equally important benefit is that people get a sense of self-worth and self-esteem from undertaking training – both because it enhances their own sense of competence and because it is a statement of confidence in them from the organization which is investing the money for the training. So training team members in order that they can develop skills which will benefit the team as a whole has a great many more benefits than may appear on the surface.

Other known human resource strategies, like 'employee of the month' schemes also have this type of effect on the individuals who received them. But if it is team pride that is in question, then obviously it's important that the team is actively featured: a 'team of the month' scheme is more effective in an organization which is trying to foster teamworking than a scheme which singles out individuals. Official communications saying 'well done', or marking positive achievements on the part of the team can have a dramatic effect on bringing the team together as a cohesive unit; and so can reports of the team's contributions to company success.

It isn't enough to rely on informal communication for knowledge of team or company success. It's true that information flies round a company very quickly, but it can become badly inaccurate in the process. The photocopier, or the staff canteen, acts as the 'village well', where people talk to their friends, pick up gossip and pass rumours around. So it is pretty naïve to assume that employees won't know something just because they have not been officially informed (although it is surprising how many managers do seem to believe it). But rumour inevitably picks up people's worries, jealousies or hopes along the way and it often becomes seriously distorted. Even if positive information seems to be well known, it needs to be communicated officially as well, if it is to have a positive effect.

There are other options for developing team pride, too, such as promoting the achievements of the main organization internally as well as externally, so that employees can see clearly what their organization has achieved and how their own efforts have contributed to the whole. This is not a new principle: one of the early Hawthorne studies featured a particularly effective informal leader who took new members around the factory so they could see where their own work fitted into the making of the final product. Members of that department took more pride in their work, and were much less likely to leave, than those in other departments.

We can see, then, how each of the various approaches to team-building can give us useful insights into the way that people work most effectively in teams. We can draw on each of them to help to create effective working teams, which can respond to the situations that they are in and deal effectively with new challenges. Effective team-building almost inevitably draws on a mixture of the various approaches and adopts several different techniques. By understanding and applying the general principles which underpin the psychological processes of belonging to a team, and of working effectively within it, we are in a good position to undertake successful team management.

SUMMARY

- Building a team involves acting within the organization as a whole, to create a situation where the team members are able to act effectively and to implement strategies which are appropriate to their task.
- Four main approaches to team-building can be detected in the organizational literature: the interpersonal approach, the role-definition approach the values approach, and the task-oriented approach.
- The interpersonal approach draws on the work of the psychologists Rogers and Berne. It aims to ensure that the team members are able to interact with one another on an honest, personal level.
- The role-definition approach draws on the various typologies of roles and group processes to make individuals aware of the style of contributions which they make in discussions; and to make teams aware of particular types of contribution which may be missing from their working practices.
- The values approach emphasizes the importance of the team having a clearly articulated set of values, which is shared by all of its members and so can direct and inform individual actions in a coherent and co-ordinated way.
- The task-oriented approach focuses on the skills and resources which the team needs to develop or assemble in order to tackle its task effectively. Interpersonal relationships and the establishment of common goals and team values are regarded as part of the required tools for effective task completion.
- The social identity approach to team-building involves developing a strong sense of team identification through establishing clear team boundaries, promoting cohesion through effective communication and encouraging pride in the team through achievement and through professionalization.

Box 3.4 **Management recommendations**

Establish definite guidelines and a clear purpose for the team, so that the team members are aware of exactly what they are supposed to be doing and what resources they have available with which to do it.

Make sure that a new team has dedicated time in which team members can meet and determine how the team will approach its goals, and what its objectives and values are. This might involve some 'time out' of the organization in a different environment.

Set up lines of communication within the organization so that the team is able to communicate its findings, insights or useful experiences to other sections of the organization.

Ensure that the team receives positive feedback and encouragement from higher levels in the organization and that it is aware that its achievements have been noted.

4 *The team and its leader*

INTRODUCTION

The relationship between a team and its leader is an interesting one, and one which has given rise to a good deal of debate. In a fully operative team, each individual member is contributing to the whole and so to single out the leader as the person responsible for the team's success would be to distort the picture by ignoring the importance of every other member of the team. Yet, on the other hand, a team without a leader can easily become direction-less and diverted from its main goals and purposes.

As with so many other aspects of social living, the issue can't be resolved by looking for simple causes. The team's achievements result from a combination of different factors. Without capable and committed team members – whether these exist beforehand or whether they develop their capabilities as part of the team – a team has no chance of working effectively. Equally, without a supportive management, a team has very little chance of success. Nor has a team working in a hostile or obstructive organizational environment – although that type of obstacle can sometimes be overcome if the individuals who make up the team already have a certain amount of power within the organization.

The team's leader, too, is a powerful determinant of the likely success of the team. A leader who is apathetic, ineffectual, openly cynical, or interpersonally hostile isn't likely to be able to maintain a positive, forward-looking team. But, on the other hand, nor is a leader who is dictatorial and dominating. The essence of a positive working team is that each individual can contribute to it, so that the team benefits from the total skills and abilities of its members. A team leader who creates a working atmosphere in which that can happen – even if it means actually standing back and handing responsibility to others from time to time – is likely to contribute a great deal to the success of the team.

The leader and the manager

Perhaps I should make it clear at this point that throughout this book, I am making a distinction between the team leader and the team's manager. The team leader belongs to the team and operates from within it. Such a leader takes responsibility for giving the team direction and vision and also, if it is appropriate, for representing the team to the rest of the organization. Obviously teams will differ in whether their leader adopts this latter function, since some teams find it worth appointing specific individuals to serve a 'diplomatic' function. But for the most part, it is the leader's responsibility to ensure that the team functions well and the leader operates from the standpoint of an involved member of the team.

The team's manager, on the other hand, is the person who has overall responsibility for that team, and possibly several others, within the overall organizational structure. In the case of an organization which emphasizes teamworking, the manager's role is mainly facilitative – ensuring that the team has access to the resources that it needs, establishing and negotiating overall organizational targets and time frames, both with the team and with other sections of the organization and keeping a watchful eye on the way that the team is progressing.

When it comes to looking at established models of leadership and how they relate to teams and teamworking, however, the boundaries between team leader and team manager can become a bit blurred. Theories are often unclear as to whether they are referring to general leaders – such as the Chief Executive Officer (CEO) of an organization; whether they are talking about managers – that is, people who have responsibility for a particular department or working sector within the organization; or whether they are talking about team leaders, who work within a particular team to establish its direction and values.

This blurring of distinctions doesn't need to trouble us too much right now, since this book has such a specific topic. What we need to do is to look briefly at the various theories of leadership and to extract from them the insights which are useful for managing teams, while leaving behind those which seem to be more relevant for other types of leadership. There is a detailed and comprehensive discussion of theories of leadership in Viv Shackleton's book *Business Leadership* (Routledge 1995) which forms a part of this series and which I would recommend to anyone interested in the topic. So here, I shall just give a very general outline of some of the main trends in leadership theory which have emerged over time, before looking at which insights may be useful for our understanding of teamworking.

HISTORICAL APPROACHES TO LEADERSHIP

As we saw in Chapter 2, much of the organizational research in the 1960s and 1970s focused on group-based structures and responsibilities, in the belief that this was the best way to tap into human social motivation. The idea was that if the working group was cohesive, then problems of work motivation and productivity would largely solve themselves. Each working group would do its own regulating, establish its own set of norms and everything would be just hunky-dory.

This approach, however, involved a rather naïve perception of the working group. While it was realistic to observe that human beings working together would naturally tend to see themselves in groups, it was not a necessary consequence that the norms and beliefs which that working group developed would automatically be the kind that would benefit the company. Nor would working groups necessarily hold progressive attitudes towards innovation and change – something that was becoming an increasing necessity in the competitive commercial environments of the 1970s and 1980s.

The group-based approach also raised a serious distinct managerial dilemma. Back in the 1930s, Mayo and his colleagues had been primarily concerned with the production workers in the Hawthorne plant, rather than with management. However, to devolve responsibility to production workers in such an extreme way was something which conflicted very deeply with the hierarchical assumptions of Western management. With one or two notable exceptions, such as Volvo in Sweden or IBM in America (and ignoring, of course, the Japanese experience) there was a widely-held belief that allowing workers any degree of autonomy would simply invite disaster. It was believed that those on the production line would not act in the best interest of the company without close and authoritative supervision.

As a result, those who tried to implement these new structures found that they were often unsuccessful, partly as a result of **self-fulfilling prophecies** (see Box 4.1). Managers who believed that workers actually needed close supervision and could not be trusted to act responsibly would convey their scepticism about the new approaches unconsciously to the work-force. They in turn, knowing they were not trusted, would not try to act in a trust-worthy manner, and so their behaviour would be taken as 'proof' that they were untrustworthy. It was a vicious cycle. Managers who did believe in the new approaches were often able to make them work within their own departments, but then encountered difficulties as their own departments interacted with the rest of the organization.

Self-fulfilling prophecies can be found everywhere in organizational life and they are a powerful influence on the way that people work. But that influence is implicit and those transmitting it are often completely unaware of what they are doing. For example, consider a manager who has a personal belief that a particular project is pointless and won't achieve anything. Unconsciously, that manager will fail to provide support and encouragement for those working on the project, and will transmit the impression that the whole business is a waste of time. The others involved in the project will pick that message up and won't put much effort into what they are doing. So the project is badly carried through and ends up a failure. The manager's initial belief becomes a self-fulfilling prophecy.

People are deeply sensitive to the non-verbal signals which form part of everyday interaction. They are part of our psychological heritage as social animals and we begin to learn them from infancy. By the time we are adult, we have become very sophisticated in reading non-verbal messages, unconsciously. Training in non-verbal communication can make us more consciously aware of some of the less subtle non-verbal signals, but it is a continual and implicit form of communication which is going on all the time. We can pick up what someone expects of us from a host of subtle cues, including their tone of voice, their posture, the timing of what they say or do, and so on.

Box 4.1   **Self-fulfilling prophecies**

Self-fulfilling prophecies are statements or beliefs which come true simply because they have been made. The idea of the self-fulfilling prophecy was first raised by a series of experiments conducted in the 1960s. One of the first of these was a study by Rosenthal and Fode in 1963, which showed that psychology students who believed that they were using 'bright' rats in a maze-running task produced better results than those who believed that their rats were genetically 'dull', even though the rats themselves had been carefully matched. But the students who believed their rats were 'bright' handled them more often and more gently, and also watched them more closely. Although they believed that they were carrying out pre-set laboratory procedures by the book and although the procedures themselves were exactly the same, the way that the students acted with the two set of animals was quite different.

In the 1960s, Rosenthal and Jacobsen showed how the beliefs held by teachers directly influenced children's academic achievement. They selected ordinary children using an IQ test and led teachers to believe that the test could detect those who would 'spurt' academically during the course of the next year. When they returned to the school a year later, the children they had named as 'spurters' had increased their grade averages and had higher places in their class. Making the prediction had influenced the children's school experiences to such an extent that they had changed their study patterns and their achievements – and yet the researchers hadn't spoken to the children at all. They had only changed the teachers' expectations.

As might be expected given its rather radical implications, the Rosenthal and Jackson study caused a furore in educational circles and its methodology was soon criticized. Objectors argued that the IQ test that they had used was not standardized for that age-range, that there was too much individual variance in the scores and that the statistical analysis was inadequate. Some replication studies were conducted, some of which confirmed the findings although others had much more equivocal results (although those didn't really replicate the original situation).

However, this was not the only source of evidence for the self-fulfilling prophecy. Rosenthal and others performed a total of 94 studies on expectancy effects, in seven different psychological areas: animal learning, human learning and ability, psychophysical judgements, reaction time, inkblot tests, laboratory interviews and person perception (Silverman 1977). In each area, they found that the unconscious expectations of the experimenters influenced the results, through subtle and unconscious non-verbal cues. Since these studies were published, the power of expectation has been widely recognized in research circles: so much so that new drugs are expected automatically to be tested using 'double-blind' procedures (where the physician doesn't know whether the patient is being given the real drug or a placebo). In organizations, too, people respond to the unconscious cues transmitted to them by their manager's expectations; so the influence of the self-fulfilling prophecy on working life is one which should not be disregarded.

This means that self-fulfilling prophecies can occur at all levels in an organization: in relationships between departments, in supervisory habits and in the decisions of the Chief Executive or the Board of Directors. And self-fulfilling prophecies can be positive too. A manager who is really convinced that a project can be a success will encourage the people working on it and help them through difficult patches, and this can carry the project through successfully. A leader who expects the best from the work-force transmits that expectation unconsciously, through tones of voice, styles of interaction and through the targets and working standards that they establish. Often, **charismatic leaders** are people who operate in this way without realizing it: they simply take it for granted that everyone wants to put their best into the job. Their work-force responds with pride at being seen so positively and so their unconscious prophecy comes true.

Leadership beliefs and leadership style

McGregor summed up this problem when he wrote about the general theories about human nature held by managers and the consequences which these had for working practice. As we saw in Chapter 1, McGregor argued that the theories held by managers fall into two camps. Theory X managers believe that human beings are essentially lazy, don't like to work and have to be closely supervised in order to make sure that they pull their weight. Theory Y managers, on the other hand, believe that human beings are essentially self-motivated, want to work and, if placed in a position where their work is appreciated, will work hard without coercion.

These beliefs, of course, are not just restricted to people at work: they actually reflect a far wider debate about human nature itself, which underlies political, educational and social practices in Western society. At work, however, these beliefs translate themselves into self-fulfilling prophecies. Workers act in accordance with the beliefs that their managers hold, and their behaviour is taken by those managers as evidence that their beliefs are correct.

Back in the 1930s, Lewin, Lippitt and White showed how the style adopted by group leaders – authoritarian, democratic or laissez-faire – produced very different types of behaviour among boys attending a hobbies club. If a leader adopted an authoritarian style, the boys would work hard while he was present but stop working as soon as they were unsupervised. A laissez-faire leader produced an unmotivated group who did little work, but a democratic leader produced a self-motivated group who worked steadily. By rotating leaders around the three groups, Lewin Lippitt and White showed that the boys' behaviour was nothing to do with their individual personalities, but entirely a product of the leadership style.

In the same way, whether a manager holds Theory X or Theory Y beliefs influences how they interact with their subordinates. That in turn means that their subordinates act according to the expectations which the manager has of them. As a result, those holding Theory X beliefs experience a work-force which is unmotivated and needs strict supervision, and do not believe that they are capable of acting responsibly. Those holding

Theory Y beliefs, on the other hand, experience a work-force which is responsible, self-motivated and hard-working.

Each, of course, takes their experiences as confirmation of the validity of their beliefs. And since organizations typically consisted of a mixture of Theory X and Theory Y managers, attempts to reorganize organizational structures into autonomous group-centred structures are only partially successful and tend to be discontinued when a Theory X manager with higher authority takes over responsibility for that section of the organization.

Incidentally, the Lewin, Lippitt and White study also received some criticism for being culturally biased. The argument was that the boys in the study were already well-adjusted to one particular style – the democratic one – because they came from middle-class homes where this was the typical style adopted by their parents. As a result, the critics argued, all of the boys performed better with the democratic leadership style and worse with the strict authoritarian one because this was what they were used to – and not because of any inherent qualities in the style itself. If they had included boys from strict, authoritarian families (not that uncommon in the 1930s) in their sample, then their findings would have been much less dramatic.

Although this is a valid criticism of the study and of the conclusions which Lewin *et al.* made, it doesn't really make a great deal of difference when we are translating its implications into the 1990s. Strictly authoritarian systems are far less common in the modern world than they were in the 1930s and people tend to take for granted their right to have a voice – even when they know that they may not have much influence. Society as a whole has moved towards the democratic style of leadership, which implies that the general implications of the Lewin study remain valid. Its sample may not have been particularly typical of its time, but it was certainly typical of ours.

THEORIES OF LEADERSHIP – AN OVERVIEW

The outcome of this was to lead to a great deal of interest in the nature of leadership itself. In the early part of this century, it was pretty well taken for granted that leadership was a purely personal quality, probably inherited, which had resulted from a combination of distinctive personality **traits**. Leadership qualities were seen as fixed within the person, and as relevant across a wide range of situations. A 'born leader' was someone who possessed leadership qualities, and there wasn't really much else to say about it.

In the 1940s, the 'great man' theory of leadership came to be challenged by what was known as the **situational** approach – an approach to understanding leadership which emphasized the particular situation that the leader was operating in. Different situations would require different qualities from the leaders involved – which meant that a leader with one set of qualities could be highly successful in one situation, but an absolute disaster in another. Organizational researchers exploring this particular dimension of leadership identified a number of different situational factors which could all influence whether the leader was effective or not. These ranged from the nature of the job itself, the history of that activity within the organization, what people or resources were available to the leader, and the nature of the relationships between the leader and those who were being led.

Gradually, researchers also began to realize that another very important factor in successful leadership was the way that the work-force viewed those in charge. Their perceptions would determine how they acted with their leaders – whether they cooperated and worked hard; whether they obeyed but didn't do anything more than was necessary, and so on. Obviously the leader's personal qualities were important to the subordinates' perceptions, but that wasn't the only thing which mattered. Subordinates were also influenced, for example, by their perceptions of the situation which existed at the time, and what they understood the leader's personal motivation to be.

This new emphasis on the cognitive aspects of leader-follower relationships continued to develop, and eventually led to a focus on the kind of **attributions** which followers make about their leaders' actions. (Why did they do that? Could they have acted differently?) So theories of leadership began to take account of the expectations of followers, as well as looking at how leaders and followers understood their own roles, and those of one another.

As research continued to develop, theories emerged which combined the study of leadership traits with an awareness of both followers' perceptions and situational conditions. These theories took the view that the leader's effectiveness arose from a combination of leader qualities and situational demands. They emphasized that whether the leader's own qualities were important was entirely contingent on the situation in which that leader was operating; so for this reason they are often referred to as **contingency** models of leadership.

Contingency models, in their turn, eventually gave way to a new set of theories of leadership models known as **transactional** theories. Transactional theories of leadership developed in the late 1970s and early 1980s and emphasized the idea that leadership arose from a kind of exchange which was going on between the leader and the led. Researchers began to explore the informal social agreements, or 'contracts', which could develop in the working situation, and also to look more deeply at the quality of interpersonal interaction which took place between leaders and their followers.

More recently, with the increased understanding of organizational factors, and in particular organizational cultures, leadership researchers began to be interested in how some leaders seem to be able to transform the expectations and assumptions of their followers. **Transformational** leaders do not just take account of these expectations and assumptions – they actively change them, so that their subordinates learn how to act in a positive way within a changing organization. Many modern theories of successful team leadership generally take a transformational approach, although this is often implicit rather than explicit.

We can see, then, that organizational research into leadership can give us some useful insights into the qualities required for successful team leadership. Different theorists have focused on different aspects of leadership – some on interpersonal interactions, some on motivation, some on expectations and some on change. Each of these theories can contribute to our general understanding of what is going on within organizations – they may not give the whole picture, but they can put another piece into the jigsaw puzzle. But they are not all equally helpful in understanding successful team leadership, as opposed to organizational management.

LEADERSHIP AND EMPOWERMENT

Another important issue surrounding effective leadership concerns the type of power possessed by the team leader and how that power is actually used. There have been a number of ways of classifying the main different types of power which are found in organizations. The most commonly used classification was the one developed by French and Raven in 1959, which is represented by the first five categories on the list in Table 4.1.

In 1991, however, Yukl and Falbe suggested that another three types of power can be seen to operate in organizations, and these are the final three categories in Table 4.1. These researchers argued that overall the eight categories could be classified into two groups. The first group is about power which depends on the

Table 4.1   Types of power (source: Shackleton 1995)

Reward power	Power which stems from the ability to control organizational resources and rewards, such as pay and bonuses.
Coercive power	Power which stems from having control over sanctions or punishments, such as reprimands or suspension.
Legitimate power	Power which stems from the organizational position held by that person, which puts them in a position of authority.
Referent power	Power which stems from subordinates liking, or respecting, the person concerned.
Expert power	Power which stems from that person being recognised as having a particular area of expertise or skill.
Information power	Power which stems from having control over information sources and information transmission in the organization.
Persuasive power	Power which stems from having an ability to convince other people as to a particular course of action or decision.
Charisma	Power which stems from personal attractiveness and transmitting a sense of dynamism, such that other people enjoy co-operating with and helping that person to achieve their goals.

individual's position within the organization, and so it includes legitimate power, reward power, coercive power, and informational power. The second group is about power which stems from the individual's own personal characteristics, and so it includes expert power, referent power, persuasive power and charisma.

There are differences in how effective these types of power are when it comes to influencing how people behave in the workplace and also when it comes to job satisfaction. Podsakoff and Schriesheim (1985) reviewed a large number of studies of power in the workplace, using the first five categories in this list and found that reward power, legitimate power and coercive power seem to be the least effective: they have either no influence or a negative influence both on how people act at work or on job satisfaction. But expert and referent power tend to produce positive outcomes – people become more involved with their work and were are inclined to leave or withdraw.

Reward systems and power

The way that employees are paid for their efforts appears to make quite a lot of difference to the way that they see power operating over their working lives. Greene and Podsakoff (1981) investigated the outcome of a change in reward systems in a paper mill. The mill had previously operated an incentive pay plan, which was largely based on production quotas. However, for various reasons it decided to change this system to one which was based on seniority – rewarding length of employment. A similar mill, also studied by the researchers, continued to operate the incentive pay plan without any changes, which allowed the researchers to make a number of direct comparisons.

When the researchers investigated how power was perceived in the two mills, they found some interesting differences. There were no changes in the second mill, which had not changed its pay practices, but in the first one, the supervisors were seen as using coercive power significantly more. They were also perceived as using reward power, referent power, and legitimate power less; also the workers' perceptions of expert power stayed much the same.

This is an interesting study because it indicates that the change to a seniority-based system was also accompanied by a more negative perception of those in authority. Effectively, they were seen as being much less likely to use the more 'positive' types of power over their workers. The incentive system, on the other hand, was accompanied by a perception of management and supervisors as less coercive, and as basing their power more on encouragement or legitimate authority.

Although in reality only the reward power factor had changed, the fact that referent and legitimate power were seen as having changed as well shows us that there is a complex relationship between how different types of power are construed by those in subordinate positions: like almost everything else involving real people, it isn't just a matter of simple, single variables acting in isolation from one another.

Power over, power to, and power from

There are other ways of classifying power, which take a rather different viewpoint. Hollander and Offerman (1990), for example, distinguish between three types of power which leaders may possess: 'power over', 'power to', and 'power from'. Each of these can be associated with leadership, but they are not all equally effective, particularly when it comes to leading a working team.

'Power over' is all about dominance, whether that dominance is implicit or explicit. It is power which is based on authority, and implies that the person holding that power is able to make other people, and in particular their subordinates, do things. It isn't, however, a particularly useful form of power when it comes to effective team leadership, since it has been shown by many researchers that depending on that kind of power undermines relationships with other members of the team and also doesn't really help the team to achieve its goals (Kipnis 1976).

'Power to' is much more useful for a team leader, since this type of power is all about enabling people to do things – having the power to make things happen. It allows the leader to act more freely and to make appropriate decisions when the situation changes unexpectedly. 'Power to' also allows the leader to empower others, by sharing power with other members of the team when it seems appropriate. This is far more useful for a team leader, since it helps the leader to foster identification with the team's goals and a sense of cohesion within the team.

The third type of power, 'power from', can also be useful to a team leader. This type of power gives the team leader the ability to fend off unwanted demands and to resist interference from other members of the organization. Being able to stick to your team's goals even when others are trying to deflect you is a vital quality; and the team leader plays an important part in maintaining it.

Empowerment and teamworking

Traditional organizational models, of course, assume that power is located with those in senior positions – that, after all, is what traditional management systems are all about. But the modern emphasis on teamworking is based on a rather different concept – that of **empowerment**. Empowerment involves a shift in power and authority within the organization, such that the people who are actually doing the work are able to take responsibility for it and to make the relevant decisions needed to carry out their work effectively.

Empowering staff isn't the same as simply delegating tasks to them. Instead, it is a management philosophy, which is all about believing that the people the organization employs have the ability, skills and motivation to do what is needed – or that they can develop those abilities, skills or motives if they are given an environment which will support it and make it worthwhile. So empowerment is about having real areas of responsibility and being able to make real decisions. These areas have boundaries, of course, as people are only empowered to take responsibility for their own work, not for the whole organization, and there is still a need for high-level management to determine direction and policy. Within these boundaries, though, the people who are actually doing the work are the people who make decisions about it.

The concept of empowerment lies at the heart of teamworking. An effective team is one which is able to take responsibility for what it is expected to do, which can make its own decisions and which can act to develop the resource-base or skill-base which it needs to undertake its task. As we've seen, the team manager's job is to facilitate that, in terms of the wider organization; but it is the team itself which organizes its tasks so that they are carried out most effectively and so it is the team which needs to be able to make the necessary day-to-day decisions.

Box 4.2   **Empowerment**

For many new managers, delegation is the hardest thing to learn. Whenever they hand over a particular task to an employee, they are plagued by worries and anxieties about whether it has been done 'properly'. As a result, they end up constantly checking on its progress, and will even take over if something isn't being done exactly the way that they think it should be. In the long run, of course, these managers get the worst of both worlds: their staff are unable to learn their jobs in a positive atmosphere, because they feel that they are being watched and criticized and as a result don't perform to the best of their abilities; while the manager ends up with just as much to do as before – if not more.

Good managers, on the other hand, have learned to overcome the feelings of anxiety which accompany delegation at first. They are aware that no two people act in exactly the same way and so do not feel threatened if they see an employee going about the task differently. Instead, they focus on the end point: was the job done and was the final result up to standard? If it was, then as long as people are working in a manner acceptable to the organization, (for example, as long as salespeople are keeping to the company's ethical selling policy) then that's fine. If an acceptable final outcome wasn't achieved, then such managers respond by discussing it with the employee and analysing the situation, to find out what training or additional skills that person will need to do it successfully in the future.

Empowerment is the key to successful delegation. There's no point expecting people to act on their own initiative if every step they have to take has to be checked or approved by someone senior to them. People rise to what is expected of them: if they are expected to act badly (which is what is communicated when every action is checked), then bad work will result. If they are given responsibility and the ability to make their own decisions, they rise to the opportunity and work well. As long as they have clear goals and are applying clear values to their work, people operate most effectively when they can make the necessary decisions about their own work.

I once became consultant to a small marketing research company, which I shall refer to as 'NewImage'. This company was entirely based around the abilities of one particularly talented director. However, he had other responsibilities as well and so could not work in the company full-time. When I first visited the company, the staff were working in very cramped offices which were physically close to their director. Since they were young people, who held him in some awe, they had fallen into the pattern of taking every single decision to him; and since he was able to deal with issues quickly, he would tackle them. However, cumulatively, the strain of working at such pressure was too much for him: his health was suffering and so was the quality of his, and their, work.

The first task was to move the staff into better accommodation, where they could operate in a more professional manner. This also had the advantage of putting them at a slight physical distance from the director, so that meetings involved a short walk rather than simply going down the corridor. The second task was to convince the director that it was worth training specific members of staff to take responsibility for particular sectors of the company's business and to hand over minor decision-making in those fields. This was done on a step-by-step basis and as each step proved itself workable, the director found himself able to hand over more responsibility.

This empowering of the staff had a considerable effect. The company developed a highly professional atmosphere: people worked hard and used their own initiative in day to day matters, while continuing to take major questions to the director. Staff turnover slowed considerably and the overall quality of the work improved.

In addition, the staff developed clearer beliefs about their own abilities to act effectively. They began to look towards a longer future with the company, discussing their future training and development and exploring new business opportunities with the director. The immediate outcome for the director was that more of his time was freed for developing other projects and for his other responsibilities. He also benefited from feeling that he had a largely self-managing team on whom he could depend, rather than a group of employees who depended on him.

Managing empowerment

Shackleton (1995) identified six aspects of a leader's role in empowerment. These six aspects are equally relevant whether the empowerment is of individual members of the work-force, or whether it is a team which is being empowered. But in this case, the leader being referred to is the person higher up in the organization who is actually empowering the team – the team's manager, rather than the leader within the team itself.

The first quality required of an empowering leader, according to Shackleton, is **respect and belief**. There is absolutely no point trying to implement an empowering system if the managers concerned have no respect for their work-force and don't actually believe that they are capable of making sensible decisions. In terms of empowering teams, successful team managers are people who believe in the potential of the team, and are able to identify and build on people's strengths as well as their weaknesses.

An important second quality which Shackleton identified is the manager's own **confidence**. Managers who feel that their own personal value to the company comes from controlling or directing other people are likely to find empowerment personally threatening. In particular, they may feel that they are risking their own jobs, since they fear that a team which is empowered to manage itself might make its manager unnecessary. However, as Shackleton points out, in the most successful cases of empowerment there is little risk of this. The leader finds new roles, through encouraging the work-force to take on more challenges, and through opening up new avenues and directions for their own work. Self-confident leaders know that their value to their organization is more than just being able to tell people what to do.

The third aspect of leadership and empowerment is all to do

with **training**. Empowering leaders need to be sensitive to the balance between respecting their employees' existing abilities and establishing training opportunities so that they can develop their potential. The most effective way, Shackleton argues, is for the leader to involve the work-force in that process, encouraging them to identify their own training needs while also fostering their self-confidence and encouraging them to become more aware of, and to apply, their existing skills.

The empowerment of staff also requires the setting of clear **boundaries**, so that everyone – both staff and managers – can be sure about what actually has been empowered, and which aspects of the work remain under higher levels of control. While they might have an input into the relevant decisions, it is simply not practical for a team to determine everything about its work: organizational policies and economic strategies always need to be left to the organizational leadership, and these will impinge on the team's targets and schedules. It may also be the case that design, marketing, or other factors are outside the team's brief. In other words, empowerment may be wide-ranging, or it may have a much narrower focus: a team may be responsible for opening up a whole new market sector, or it may simply be responsible for the production of a particular section of an aircraft. What is important, though, is that the team's manager has established the boundaries of the team's responsibilities, clearly and unambiguously.

Empowering a team or a group of employees almost always means that the team or working group will need more **information** than they have needed before. Making decisions and taking responsibility involves knowing what the relevant factors are: doing as you are told needn't mean knowing anything much at all. The key to successful empowerment in this respect, Shackleton argues, is that the team itself is able to specify the information that it needs, when it will need the information, and which of their members will need to have it. The manager's task, in this respect, is to facilitate the transfer of this information and make sure that the team is provided with what it needs.

The sixth factor which Shackelton identifies in managing empowerment is all to do with the **rate of progress** that the team achieves. Again, a manager needs to strike a balance between allowing the team to find its own feet and determine its own rate of progress, and pushing them to ensure that organizational schedules are met. The manager will need to work closely with the team's leader on this one, to ensure that the team has practical working objectives which can help the team members to know whether they are working effectively to schedule or not.

As we can see, there is a rather different model of leadership underlying these six factors than could have been suggested by the top-down theories that we looked at earlier. Empowerment presents a model of leadership which is all about listening to the work-force, encouraging them, coaching them where necessary and building up their self-confidence through pointing out and setting up small successes. The manager becomes the 'facilitator' who helps the team to get on with its work, rather than the 'boss' who tells everyone what they should be doing and when.

Does a self-managing team need a leader?

All of this, of course, raises the question of whether a team needs a a leader at all. If the managerial principles of empowerment and the self-managing team are fully implemented within the organization then, some researchers argue, there is little need for a leader in the team. The individuals in the team will be able to structure their own work, make their own decisions, and operate together to be effective without needing someone to tell them what to do.

In fact, there has been a considerable amount of recent debate about whether leaders are important at all. In 1987, Meindl and Ehrlich argued that the whole concept of leadership in business has been over-romanticized and that people have tended to attribute organizational success to leaders where in reality other factors, in particular the quality of the working groups which those leaders had under them, were what had really mattered. Because the idea of the dynamic, charismatic leader is such an attractive model, Meindl and Ehrlich argued, organizational research is biased towards looking for leadership characteristics and so makes leaders seem more important than they really are.

Following on from this, Meindl (1992) argued that the bias towards looking at leadership has meant that organizational research has largely ignored questions about the quality and influence of subordinates and working groups. The whole concept of leadership, Meindl argued, needs to be re-invented, so as to take into account the way that 'followers' go about their work and the relationship between them and the leader. Box 4.3 discusses a

Box 4.3   **Are leaders necessary?**

The question of whether leaders are actually necessary is an interesting one. Clearly, leaders are important in establishing new directions and new ways of working. But the idea of positive management nowadays is to facilitate self-motivation and empowerment on the part of individuals. It follows, then, that once that way of working has been established, the group should be pretty capable of functioning without the leader, although the leader may still have an important long-term role to play.

This was illustrated very clearly by a team of busy secretaries, each of whom serviced a different department in the educational faculty of a large university. The team had been established by a highly competent administrator, who had brought together what had previously been a number of rather haphazard departmental structures. Each of the secretaries had responsibility for her own department and they covered for one another if anyone happened to be away. The workload was heavy and extremely pressured at certain times of year.

The administrator operated a hands-off, supportive management policy, encouraging the secretaries to develop an ordered, systematic approach to their work and making time for the necessary reorganization which that involved. He saw his job as facilitating, or enabling, rather than as dictating. Under his guidance the secretaries' work became ordered, smooth and competent. However, after three years, organizational policy dictated that faculty administrators should be moved around and so he had to leave.

The new administrator had a quite different style. He was an organizational 'bully' – obsequious to those above him, obstructive with the professional and technical staff of the faculty (who operated under a different line management system) and domineering with his subordinates, particularly the secretarial team. Faced with threats and unpleasantness where they had previously encountered encouragement and support, morale in the team declined rapidly.

However, despite this, the teamwork and autonomous approach established by the previous administrator had become a working habit and could not be totally undone. On a day to day basis, the secretaries functioned as efficiently as they had before and when the administrator was away, they worked as hard as they had ever done. (When he was present, this was more difficult, as he tended to interrupt their work with dominance activities of one form or another). The difference was that they were frequently emotionally upset by the administrator and as a result had few reserves for the little extra requests which came from the departmental staff – although the code of helpfulness which had grown up ensured that they always attempted to do as much as possible.

According to any simplistic indicators, then, the change of leader had actually made very little difference to the way that the secretaries worked. They continued to be efficient, thorough and reliable, and to help one another out. In the long term, though, innovation and morale suffered badly, stress levels were high, and – perhaps more importantly – most of them began to look around for other jobs. The change of leader had not affected how well their day to day work was performed, but it had considerable long-term implications.

real-life example where a change of leadership might have been expected to make a dramatic difference, but in the long term simply meant that the employees found ways of getting on with their work just as efficiently as before.

Of course nobody, not even Meindl, doubts that there are leaders who can make a considerable difference to how people work. It has been demonstrated time and again that leaders can transform an unproductive, negative working group or even a whole organization in to one with a high level of professionalism and a competent, efficient style of working. But once people have learned to operate in that way, it is open to question how important the leader is in continuing the process. Meindl's attempt to open up this debate attracted considerable opposition from other organizational researchers, but it is a valid question to ask, even if asking it means that we come to the conclusion that team leaders do have an important function after all.

Are self-managing teams really self-managing?

In terms of team management the issue of how necessary leadership is has also been raised, but this time in a slightly different context. Here, the debate is about self-managing teams – the type of team that we have been discussing, which is largely able to determine its own way of working and make its own decisions. Manz (1992) argued that what were generally called self-managing teams were often not really all that self-managing. In fact, management practices and organizational constraints meant that these teams were much more limited than they might appear. Manz argued that organizations could go much further in this process, moving from self-managing teams to self-leading teams. Such teams would not only be able to make decisions about their work, but would also be empowered to influence strategic issues about what they do and why they do it.

Shipper and Manz (1992) described a large organization where this type of policy had been put into practice. This company had set itself up as a whole conglomerate of self-developing teams, without managers or bosses. It did, however, have a very strong organizational culture, which was widely shared and involved a great deal of working with semi-independent associates rather than employees. Effectively, the organization which they were describing was one which took the teamwork philosophy to its limits, and seemed to make it work. But it was a long way from being typical of most organizations.

For most organizations, though, such an extreme approach wouldn't be seen as particularly desirable; and there are also questions about how such an organization would continue to function over time. Manz appeared to be taking the view that self-management should mean complete autonomy, but many other researchers and organizational psychologists would question whether that is in fact a valuable thing. For many people, working within a coherent structure but having autonomy in their own particular sector is much more desirable than operating with such a wide range of strategic levels.

And there is also the question of getting from here to there. Laiken (1994) described self-managed teams which are expected to function without management guidance, and without leaders. These teams, Laiken pointed out, frequently flounder, becoming bogged down in minor conflicts, directionless and unproductive.

Such teams are found in organizations whose managers have taken the teamworking philosophy to extremes, without considering that the extreme may not always be the most desirable option. They establish the teams and expect them to find their own direction, but they don't offer the kind of facilitation which helps the team to develop itself.

Laiken argued that the principle of the leaderless team should be seen as an eventual end-point, not a beginning. At first, in an organization which is shifting towards self-managing teams, people will need structure and guidance. They will also, as we've seen, need clear leadership within the team and facilitation from the manager responsible for it. Within those boundaries, teams can function well and for many organizations that will be as much as is required. Organizations which wish to take it further should establish these types of self-managing teams first and then gradually build on the skills which people have developed to widen their areas of responsibility. It is a process of development and guidance which takes time, not one which can be adopted instantly.

LEADING A TEAM

When we look at research into leadership and into the role of leadership in self-managed teams, we can see that modern approaches to team leadership are likely to be framed within a different set of assumptions from earlier leadership theories. The modern approach assumes that the team is perceived as composed of autonomous individuals, who may or may not actively choose to co-operate, and certainly will not do so unless they can see a good reason why they should. So although modern approaches do draw on the insights provided by traditional theories of leadership, they also have developed their own principles, integrating traditional insights with practical experience in the field and advances in psychological understanding.

One of the clearest expositions of the modern approach to team leadership was put forward by Katzenbach and Smith (1993), who identified six principles of good team leadership – or, to be more precise, six things which good team leaders do. The principles are listed in Table 4.2, but we will discuss each one in a bit more detail here. In this model, the first principle of team leadership is that good team leaders will always keep the purpose, goals and

Table 4.2   Principles of team leadership (adapted from Katzenbach and Smith 1994)

Good team leaders:

1. Keep the purpose, goals and approach of the team relevant and meaningful.
2. Build commitment and confidence in team members.
3. Strengthen the mix and level of skills in the team.
4. Manage relationships with outsiders, including removing obstacles from the team's path.
5. Create opportunities for other members of the team.
6. Do real work.

approach of their team relevant and meaningful. In other words, they help their team to clarify their aims and their values, and make sure that the team members don't get diverted into courses of action which will lead them away from these.

But there is also an issue about how good team leaders go about doing this. Katzenbach and Smith draw a distinction between hierarchical leaders who aim to control their working groups and team leaders. Although team leaders steer their team towards its goals, they don't try to drive them. Indeed, Katzenbach and Smith argue that leaders who specify too much of the team's purpose, goals and approach – particularly early on in the team's life – will threaten the individual commitment of team members, by devaluing the team's ability to make its own decisions and adopt responsibility for them. A good team leader believes in what the team is all about and so is able to resist the temptation to jump in and control everything. They are able to be patient and take a back seat as the team as a whole works these issues out.

The second principle is that good team leaders work to build up the commitment and confidence of each individual team member, as well as the team as a whole. They take up opportunities to show the team how positively they have acted; they encourage people to value each other's abilities and skills and they show that they appreciate it when their team members act on their own initiative. By doing this, they help to encourage the individuals who make up the team to become or remain committed to it, as well as encouraging the development of responsibility and autonomy.

Another task of the good team leader is to be continually vigilant about the team's skills. Team leaders constantly aim to strengthen the mix and level of the skills in the team, because no team can be successful if it has a serious 'skill gap' between the skills which it needs and the skills it actually has. So it is important that the team leader is constantly appraising what team members can do and spotting opportunities for development. Just carrying out a skill appraisal when the team is first set up isn't enough, because the team's activities will be changing all the time and the team's skills have to develop with them.

Effective team leaders identify the likely future skill demands on the team and try to prepare for the future, so that when further challenges come forward the team is ready. They may do this by making sure that someone gets the practice that they need in a particular role, so that they can consolidate their knowledge and acquire expertise; they may shift assignments or roles to allow individual team members to develop new skills in a new field; or they may build on the personal interests of individual team members through training. Or, if the skill gap can't be addressed that way, they may bring new people into the team, who have skills which complement the others.

The fourth thing which good team leaders do is to manage relationships with outsiders – including removing obstacles from the team's path. As a general rule, it is the team leader who is responsible for relationships between the team and 'outsiders' – whether they be other members of the organization, the general public or those from other organizations. Even if the team shares this responsibility, outsiders will often approach the team leader, and assume that that person manages the team's external contacts. So an important task of the team leader is to smooth the path, so that the team can carry out its work unhindered.

This smoothing can take several forms. Sometimes, it means that the team leader needs to shield the team members from the kind of gratuitous criticism or managerial pressures which would lower the quality of their work. Sometimes, it means interceding on the team's behalf with higher management, when the organization puts apparently insuperable obstacles in the way. Sometimes, too, it means communicating clearly about the team's values, aims and objectives, so that others in the organization will gain a better understanding of what the team is doing and why.

Effective team leaders also create opportunities for others. One of the differences between someone who is leading a team and someone who is managing a working group, according to Katzenbach and Smith, is that the team leader puts the team above their own ego, and so doesn't automatically grab all of the best opportunities and credit. By stepping back and allowing other team members to take on responsibilities, or to learn how to perform new tasks, the team leader creates opportunities for each team member to develop. And by doing so, they also build up each individual's commitment to the team.

The sixth of Katzenbach and Smith's principles of team leadership is that team leaders do real work. They make sure that everyone on the team, including themselves, contributes roughly the same amount. Furthermore, they don't automatically delegate difficult or nasty tasks to others, but show their commitment to the team by taking these on themselves. By doing this, they are showing in their actions – always the most convincing type of demonstration – that they really do believe in the team, and are prepared to do their utmost to make it work. That type of example makes it very difficult for other team members to do less.

What team leaders don't do

Katzenbach and Smith also identify two things that good team leaders never do. The first of these is that they don't blame – they recognize that mistakes do happen sometimes. So when errors do occur, good team leaders deal with them without increasing the pressure on the individual concerned. That doesn't mean that they just let it pass: instead, they focus on encouraging the team and the individuals concerned to learn from those mistakes, so that they won't happen again. But they don't spend time blaming or reprimanding that person. After all, in a committed team both success and failure are team events, not individual ones.

Good team leaders use mistakes as a way of looking at the situation to see what lessons can be learned. They look for constructive ways of overcoming the setback. These might be individual ones, such as securing additional training for that person or making sure that the person has an opportunity to do something else challenging and well, soon, so that their working confidence doesn't become eroded. Alternatively, they might be team-focused solutions: ways that the team as a whole can overcome the skill gap which has been revealed, or seeing whether new patterns of working or communication need to be established so that the weakness in the system (not the person) is taken care of.

The other thing which good team leaders never do, according the Katzenbach and Smith, is to excuse away shortfalls in the team's performance. Instead, they acknowledge that the team has not managed to achieve what it set out to do and, again, look constructively for ways to sort out the problem. This is very different from 'normal' organizational practice, in which failure is generally punished and so there is an incentive to explain it away. By taking responsibility for the team's failures as well as its successes, the leader consolidates the sense of teamwork and commitment of the team members and encourages each team member to work freely, and to the best of their ability. It also fosters a constructive approach to problem-solving, rather than one which simply ignores the problem's existence.

TEAM LEADERSHIP AND SOCIAL IDENTIFICATION

As we can see from Katzenbach's principles, the modern team leader combines both transactional and transformational qualities. Those principles concerned with creating opportunities for other members of the team, participating in the team's work and managing relationships with outsiders, emphasize the transactional nature of team leadership; while those concerned with building up the team members' commitment and confidence, keeping goals and aims firmly in everyone's mind, and strengthening the mix and level of skills in the team emphasize transformational qualities.

By acting according to these principles, the team leader is making sure that the team stays on-target and that team members don't become demoralized or sidetracked. But there is more to it than that. What these principles also do is to enable the team leader to build up and maintain a strong sense of **social identification** between members of the team. The team leader, through actions as well as words, is creating a sense of the team as a special unit, with distinctive abilities and skills, differentiated from other people in the organization.

In addition, the team leader who acts according to these principles is encouraging a sense of **cohesion** between members. By making opportunities for everyone to contribute, by making sure that the team has the skills needed for the job and – most importantly – by joining in the work personally, the team leader makes sure that all the team members can feel that this special group works together, as a unit, and that they have their own place in it.

And, of course, the team leader who carries out their job in this way is creating a climate in which team members can feel proud of belonging to their team. Smoothing over dealings with outsiders and obstacles reduces opportunities for negative or disparaging interactions with others, while building commitment and confidence on the part of the team members and enhancing their professionalism through skill development both serve to increase their personal confidence. So as a result of the way that the team's leader goes about their own task, belonging to the team becomes something which is distinctive, cohesive and enhances self-esteem: the perfect conditions for positive social identification.

SUMMARY

- A team's leader operates within the team to ensure that it works with clarity and direction. A team's manager works outside the team and facilitates the team's operations by making resources available and setting targets. Both undertake some aspects of the leadership role.
- Leadership beliefs can result in self-fulfilling prophecies, which can influence how employees behave. Theories of leadership have included trait theories, situational theories, attributional approaches, contingency models, transactional theories and transformational approaches.
- Various types of power operating within organizations have been identified. They can be roughly classified into power which derives from the person's position within an organization and power which derives from the individual's personal characteristics.
- Empowerment is an important concept in teamworking. It is a management philosophy which assumes that day-to-day decisions about work are best undertaken by those who are doing that work.
- There has been some debate about how necessary leaders are, but the consensus is that although teams can take on a great deal of autonomy, leaders help to give them direction and to keep them targeted on their work.

- Principles of team leadership include keeping goals clear, building confidence, commitment and skills, managing external relationships, creating opportunities for team members and doing real work.
- The principles of team leadership draw on the underlying psychological mechanisms of social identification, by encouraging cohesion between group members, establishing a sense of professionalism or working competence, and so allowing people to identify with their team and feel proud of belonging to it.

Box 4.4   **Management recommendations**

Consider each of Shackleton's six principles of empowerment in turn, looking at how they have been involved in implementing and managing the team.

Make sure that the goals and targets of the team are clear, so that all team members know what the team has to achieve and in what sort of time-scale. Break the overall goal down into a number of smaller, manageable targets.

Work towards developing a set of sub-goals or targets which can be used to to identify training needs within the team, as well as encouraging team members' commitment to the overall goal.

Create opportunities through which individual team members can take on responsibility and contribute to the overall task at hand. Use these to help to build up self-confidence, which in turn will contribute to a professional and committed approach.

Streamline obstructive organizational processes which cause delays in the transmission of information or the implementation of reforms.

---

5 *Evaluating team performance*

The question of evaluating team performance is a challenging one, and it is one which has been addressed on a number of different levels. At one level, evaluating teams can mean measuring their characteristics, and seeing how team members respond to particular psychometric instruments. At another level, it might mean using reference criteria such as the team performance curve to plot how well a given team seems to be doing. Evaluating team performance might mean assessing the quality of the team's decision-making, and ensuring that it has not become influenced by damaging or negative factors. And evaluating team performance invariably means considering the questions of reward and incentives: should one use team-based reward systems for rewarding team efforts, or will that lead to social loafing and other undesirable consequences?

PSYCHOMETRIC APPROACHES TO TEAM MEASUREMENT

Questionnaires and inventories have always been a popular approach in management circles, so not surprisingly, there have been a number of attempts to develop such tools for measuring and evaluating teams. Some psychometric approaches to team measurement have been specifically designed to investigate team working, while others have been adaptations of existing individual tests, emphasizing measurement of the role characteristics required for teamworking.

The Belbin team role self-perception inventory

In Chapter 2, we saw how Belbin (1981) had developed a model of eight team roles, derived from observations of general managers on training courses. The managers concerned would undertake a particular simulation exercise, the Executive Management Exercise, as part of their course. They had taken the 16PF personality test and the Watson Glaser Critical Thinking Appraisal beforehand, and their behaviour during the exercise was observed, using a system based on Bales' interaction analysis (see Chapter 2). Belbin derived the set of team roles from the information provided by these measures, and also produced a self-report questionnaire, known as the Belbin Team Role Self-Perception Inventory (BTRSPI).

The BTRSPI rapidly became a very popular method of evaluating team roles and was widely adopted by a number of commercial organizations and management consultancies, and used for training courses as well as team-building and development. However, in 1993, Furnham et al. published a detailed psychometric evaluation of the BTRSPI and found a number of weaknesses (Furnham, Steele and Pendleton 1993a). One of the problems was that the questions were vague and inconsistent. For example, respondents were asked to specify their typical behaviour in situations such as 'when I am involved in a project with other people . . . '. Since this type of questioning is so general, it can lead to misunderstandings and is likely to produce very inconsistent results – and the more experience people have of working in diverse teams, the more unreliable those results are likely to be.

Another problem which they identified was that the BTRSPI was an **ipsative test**, which was being used as if it was a normative one. Ipsative tests are ones which assess a person's stronger and weaker traits – or in this case, the roles people may be more or less likely to adopt. The problem is that ipsative tests give results which only relate to the particular individual who has taken the test and can't really be used to compare one person with another (Johnson, Wood and Blinkhorn 1988). This is because of the way that ipsative tests work. In an ipsative test, scores are distributed between the items in the test in such a way that they always make up the same total. Stronger characteristics get more points from the pool, so this automatically means that weaker characteristics are allocated less. For instance, in the BTSPRI, respondents are given seven situations. For each one they are asked to distribute ten points between eight sentences which describe their most likely behaviour in those situations.

Although this way of assessing characteristics can be very useful in giving us insight into an individual person's strengths and weaknesses, it doesn't really tell us very much about how they compare with other people. If someone scores highly on, say, shaper and plant roles, but low on monitor-evaluator or chairman ones, this tells us which roles they personally are best at. Another person, though, might score only moderately on the shaper role – because they were particularly good at something else – and yet still be better at it than the other person was. Ipsative scores can demonstrate our own characteristics and preferred styles, but they don't provide objective data which can be used to compare individuals with other people.

Furnham *et al.* also argued that the BTRSPI had not been properly evaluated as a psychometric test. There was no published evidence of its reliability (whether the test gave consistent answers when it was administered to the same people at different times), of its validity (whether it really measured what it claimed to measure), or of its dimensionality (how the different roles and role-measurements related to one another). Each of these are fundamental requirements for a valid psychometric test and yet a search of the published literature had produced virtually nothing of this kind.

Belbin (1993a) responded to this criticism by arguing that the Belbin Team Role Self-Perception Inventory had never been marketed as a psychometric test. It had been included in the Appendix to a book about team management, as a quick and easy way of indicating their own team roles to managers who had read the book. The formally marketed test was what Belbin described as a 'more robust way of assessing the potential team role contribution of individuals', known as Interplace (Belbin Associates 1988). This was based on the same model, but used additional sources of data. However, Furnham *et al.* (1993b) pointed out that since the BTRSPI was actually used as the basis for organizational decision-making, it was important that it was actually valid for its purpose. Moreover, they argued, their criticisms also appeared to apply to the Interplace model, which was marketed as a psychometric tool.

Furnham, Steele and Pendleton (1993a) conducted three studies designed to investigate the reliability and dimensionality of the Belbin Team Role Self-Perception Inventory. Their results indicated that there was a considerable degree of unreliability in the test items, and also that there seemed to be little connection between the dimensionality of the test items which was revealed by factor analysis, and the descriptions of their relationship which had been suggested in Belbin's own writing. In other words, Belbin had suggested that some of the team roles linked together, but the empirical analysis didn't give much evidence for those connections.

These studies, however, were rather more controversial than the critical analysis which the researchers had made, partly because of the way that Furnham *et al.* used the BTRSPI itself. As other researchers have shown (Johnson, Wood and Blinkhorn 1988), it is inappropriate to use factor analysis on an ipsative test, because it doesn't have independent measuring scales – the size of the scores on one item will have been affected by the size of the scores on the others. To take account of that, two of Furnham, Steele and Pendleton's three studies had used a 'de-ipsativized' version of the test. This gave results which were quite different from the third study, which had used the original test. Furnham *et al.* suggested that this was evidence that the BTRSPI was unreliable, but Belbin (1993a) argued that the test had been changed so much by rendering it non-ipsative that it was hardly a fair evaluation. Although Furnham *et al.* challenged this point too, their case here was weaker. And since they themselves had observed that it was inappropriate to use factor analysis on ipsative test data, their third study was not really a valid assessment even on their own terms.

The 16PF and the OPQ

The 16PF and the OPQ are well-known psychometric tests which are used extensively in job selection and career assessment. They are questionnaire-style tests, which produce personality profiles rather than single scores, and both of them have been extensively researched and validated. The 16PF, as its name suggests, measures 16 personality factors in adult personality and is used in clinical and educational settings as well as by occupational psychologists. The OPQ measures 30 separate aspects of behaviour, interests and personality characteristics in a work context.

Interestingly, although these tests are essentially measures of individual personality, they have also been used to measure team roles. The 16PF was used, as we have seen, in Belbin's original research into teamwork and has been used as data in team management studies ever since 1948 (Dulewicz 1995). The OPQ, too, has been related to Belbin's team roles, with norms which were provided from the assessments of over 1,000 managers and professionals (Mabey and Hunter 1986). Each test's publisher produces a programme whereby those using the test can produce team role profiles from the individual test scores.

Although Belbin (1993b) argued that the precise measure used to assess team role was 'almost incidental', Dulewicz (1995) suggested that it seemed to be becoming increasingly common for the results obtained from one set of tests to contradict those obtained from another. But this was anecdotal evidence and not particularly trustworthy. What was needed was some explicit reseach evidence to see how the tests related to Belbin's eight team roles. As a result, Dulewicz conducted a study of 100 managers, each responsible for an average of 246 people, which investigated how reliable and how similar the teamwork measures obtained from the 16PF and the OPQ were.

The correlations between the 16PF team roles and the OPQ team roles are given in Table 5.1. As we can see from the table, for the most part the two tests do correlate in their assessments of the team roles and their correlations are statistically significant. The exception is the Monitor-evaluator role, which is not a

Table 5.1 Correlations between 16PF team roles and OPQ team roles (adapted from Dulewicz 1995)

Team role	Correlation coefficient	Significance level
Plant	.27	$p<.01$
Shaper	.49	$p<.01$
Co-ordinator	.28	$p<.01$
Resource Investigator	.66	$p<.01$
Team worker	.33	$p<.01$
Implementer	.40	$p<.01$
Completer-finisher	.42	$p<.01$
Monitor-evaluator	.13	NS
(N=100)		

significant correlation. Dulewicz suggested that part of the explanation for the ME scale finding could be because the 16PF has a reasoning scale, while the OPQ doesn't. The presence or absence of a reasoning scale could make quite a difference to how well the two psychometric tests agree on this particular team role, since the ME role involves a considerable amount of reasoning and evaluation.

There is, then, some evidence that the team role scoring systems based on these two major personality tests do agree with one another. But this type of psychometric evaluation leaves unanswered a very different question. How far can psychometric evaluation based on individual profiles actually address the more subtle aspects of teamworking – and in particular, the organizational context within which the team operates? Ideally, too, such measurement would also need to take into account the way that the social dimension of the team experience contributes to make team achievements greater than those of the individuals comprising the team. The fundamental assumption of the team roles approach is that once the appropriate team roles have been sorted out, everything else will just fall into place. But the social dynamics of interpersonal interaction are not often that simple.

PRINCIPLES OF TEAM MEASUREMENT

Dyer (1984), in a review of research into teamwork and training, argued that many teamwork measures were unreliable, unnecessarily complex, insensitive to the subtleties of teamworking and measured variables which were actually irrelevant to the process. The lack of appropriate techniques for measuring team performance, Dyer argued, meant that most research into teamworking suffered from the weaknesses of the tools which were used to evaluate the team and so was not able to provide an accurate, or even halfway accurate, picture of teamworking.

Baker and Salas (1992) identified a set of six principles for evaluating teamwork skills. The first was 'There's nothing so practical as a good theory' – that understanding teamwork requires a sound theory, since it is the theory underpinning the measure which will dictate what is actually evaluated. They called the second 'What you see may not be what you get', by which they meant that both situations and maturation influence teamwork skills, so only observations in a variety of settings and over time can give an accurate picture of which teamwork skills are the robust, significant ones.

The third principle was 'There is no escaping observation' – in that it is simply not practical to assess teamworking fully from self-report measures or second-hand accounts. Since team members are unlikely to be fully aware of the social dynamics taking place as they work, some kind of direct observation will always be required. The fourth principle emphasized the need for widespread application: teamwork measures need to be developed, applied and evaluated in a variety of different types of teams and settings. Without this, it will not be possible to refine and develop the theory and the measuring instruments, or to identify fundamental mechanisms and factors.

Baker and Salas's fifth and sixth principles concern the need for psychometric rigour. The fifth is that both judges and measures of teamwork must be reliable. That reliability, they argue, needs to be assessed at two levels: first, at the level of inter-rater reliability, since observers are so important to the overall evaluation (principle 3); and second, at the level of internal consistency and stability over time. Their sixth principle is concerned with validating the measure thoroughly, so that users can be sure that it provides accurate information for evaluation of teamworking and for training.

These six principles may appear demanding, but there does seem to be at least one psychometric measure of teamworking which appears to conform to all six of these criteria – and, moreover, was *not* developed by Baker and Salas! This is the Team Climate Inventory, developed by Anderson and West and published in 1994 by NFER-Nelson.

The team climate inventory

The theoretical basis for the team climate inventory originated in a three-year research programme into work group climate and innovativeness. As a result of this and an extensive knowledge basis from previous research projects, a theoretical model of organizational climate for innovation was developed by West (1990). As the research continued, this theoretical model formed the basis for the development of the Team Climate Inventory.

West's model had identified four factors as being crucial to organizational innovation, which we will be discussing in more depth in Chapter 7. The four factors are participative safety, support for innovation, vision and task orientation, and these generated the elements in the Team Climate Inventory (TCI). In addition, a social desirability scale was included, as a fifth factor. This allowed the users of the TCI to detect when respondents were trying to present themselves or their team in a better light than might really be justified. Each of the TCI scales was sub-divided into other measures, assessing different aspects of the team's working climate, as shown in Table 5.2.

The Team Climate Inventory went through a rigorous procedure of validation, reliability checks, and application in a range of settings (e.g. Anderson and West, 1994b). Agrell and Gustafson (1994) reported on a longitudinal study of the Team Climate Inventory in Sweden, where it was administered to 16 work teams, with a total of 124 respondents. The Swedish version of the inventory was translated into Swedish by two professional translators and then re-translated back into English by an English speaker with fluent Swedish, in order to make sure that the items remained substantially the same. The questionnaire was completed by all the team members and each team was also rated

Table 5.2 Scales and sub-scales of the Team Climate Inventory (source: Anderson and West 1994a)

Scale	*Sub-scale*
Participative Safety	Information sharing
	Safety
	Influence
	Frequency of interaction
Support for Innovation	Articulated support
	Enacted support
Vision	Clarity
	Perceived value
	Sharedness
	Attainability
Task Orientation	Excellence
	Appraisal
	Ideation
Social Desirability	Social aspect
	Task aspect

independently for their innovativeness, quality and quantity. The outcomes were then subjected to a variety of reliability and validity analyses.

Agrell and Gustafson found that their findings supported the results which Anderson and West (1994b) had obtained from their study of 27 NHS management teams in Britain. The implication that this team measuring instrument was robust enough to be able to move across cultures led to its translation into a number of other languages, and the implications so far seem to be that its cross-cultural validity is promising. The Team Climate Inventory has also been used extensively as the basis for team-building projects (see Box 5.1).

The main strength of the TCI as a team measurement tool is the way that it is so firmly based: first on a thoroughly researched and tested theory, and second on validation and reliability data collected from its application in the field, in a range of different settings. While many of the existing checklists and questionnaires for team functioning have derived simply from practical observation, the TCI has been derived from practical observation refined and articulated with psychometric rigour. As a result, it does, at least at the present time, promise to be one technique for evaluating teamwork which has some potential for actually assessing how teams are able to operate in an effective and innovative manner.

Box 5.1 Using the TCI for teambuilding

Anderson and West (1996) reported two instances where the Team Climate Inventory was used explicitly as the basis for a team building exercise. Both teams concerned high-level hospital management, operating within the British National Health Service, and the studies were conducted in early 1990 – a time when the NHS was experiencing a considerable amount of government-imposed change and all hospitals were under pressure to change their working practices.

The first team, which the researchers imaginatively called Team A, was the senior management team of an acute hospital, with a total of 170 patient beds and 970 medical and administrative staff. There were five individuals in the management team, which was a close-knit group led by a highly charismatic leader.

The Team Climate Inventory showed that this team scored highly on participative safety, support for innovation and task orientation. However, they also scored highly on the social desirability scale, which implied that the other high scores needed to be taken with a pinch of salt. In particular, and not uncommonly, there was more articulated support for innovation then enacted support. Even more importantly, the team scored lower on the Vision scale: there was little clarity over the team's objectives and some doubts as to how valuable those objectives were.

The intervention from the research team began by giving the team direct feedback on their TCI profile, in order to probe and test the overly positive presentation indicated by the social desirability response. Once the reseachers were satisfied that the team really did agree with its self-presentation (or most of it), the second part of the intervention focused on the development of a stronger and more clearly shared vision, which could also be translated into shared objectives.

Team B was responsible for a large general hospital, with roughly 300 patients' beds and over 3100 staff. Since the hospital was semi-autonomous, the management was able to make all decisions relating to the resource allocation within the hospital which, unsurprisingly, led to a considerable degree of political intrigue and lobbying for funds. The management team consisted of eight members and was led by a Chief Executive who was extremely politically adept, and always retained the final decision over resource allocation.

The TCI profile for Team B was very different from that of Team A. There were lower scores on all of the aspects of participative safety, apart from frequency of interaction, on enacted support for innovation and on task orientation. However, the team scored more highly on the vision scale and low on social desirability. Overall, the picture was of minimal trust between team members in spite of regular contact, of little practical support for innovation despite rhetoric in its favour, and of very little self-evaluation among the team members.

Based on these results, the research team's intervention began with a series of non-threatening exercises to encourage interpersonal trust and co-operation. This involved working away from the hospital for a few days, to avoid pressures from work. The exercises were designed to emphasize the need for collaborative efforts in co-operative task performance, in order to achieve the superordinate goals of the organization. A second part of the intervention involved highlighting the question of support for innovation and initating discussions and action planning designed to increase enacted support.

Unfortunately, it was not possible to use the TCI to identify explicit differences in team climate resulting from the interventions, since its items had formed such a strong basis for discussion and feedback in both teams. However, both teams demonstrated moderate improvements in their work-related behaviours and reported that they had found the TCI feedback very useful, even though it had been discomfiting at times.

(Source: Anderson and West 1996)

THE TEAM PERFORMANCE CURVE

Katzenbach and Smith (1993), in their book on high-performance teams, put forward an entirely different approach to evaluating team performance. This one does not adopt psychometric measures at all, but instead focuses on the impact of the team within the organization and its value in achieving the team task effectively. Katzenbach and Smith propose looking at team effectiveness by assessing where any particular team would fall on the 'team performance curve' (Figure 5.1).

In this model, the difference between the **working group** and the team is that the working group does not have any particular need to develop and amplify its performance. But working groups

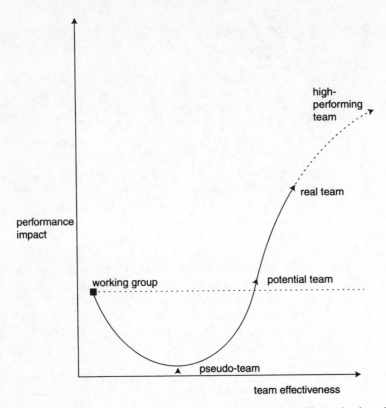

Figure 5.1 The team performance curve (source: Katzenbach and Smith 1993)

aren't necessarily a bad thing, and Katzenbach and Smith emphasize that for some organizations, they are entirely appropriate.
People participate in a working group to share information, to
make decisions and to co-ordinate practices. The difference
between that and the team is that the emphasis is always on
enabling each individual to undertake their own area of responsibility. There is no shared responsibility and no particular need to
establish it.

A **real team**, by contrast, is a small number of people who are
all jointly committed to a common purpose. They have shared
goals and consider each member of the team to be equally accountable for what the team achieves, as well as for the general work-

ing approach that the team adopts. That doesn't mean, though, that everyone in the group is regarded as being the same. A real team of this kind, according to Katzenbach and Smith, will consist of people who have complementary skills and who are also ready to learn new ones if the task demands it. But because they work together, what they are able to achieve is far more than they could have achieved if they had operated on an individual, or on a working-group basis.

There are a number of pitfalls, though, in moving from a working group to a real team. One of them is the danger of simply becoming a **pseudo-team** – a group of people who are called, or who call themselves, a team and might have that potential, but who don't actually try to co-ordinate what they are doing or establish collective responsibility at all. Many senior management teams are of this kind: although their members may call themselves a team, in reality they act on a purely individual level and are concerned only with their own departments and responsibilities. They are a team in name only – a pseudo-team. And many organizations which move into teamworking without really thinking through what is involved end up creating organizations consisting of pseudo-teams rather than real ones. As the diagram shows, pseudo-teams can be actually less effective than working groups.

The **potential team** is a rather more optimistic halfway stage between the working group and the real team. This is a group which can see that there is a real need to improve performance and which is really trying to do something about it. They are held back, though, mainly by a lack of clarity about shared goals and purposes and also by working practices which emphasize individual responsibilities and make it difficult to establish truly co-ordinated operations. Given the right type of leadership and management, a potential team can make the change into a real team relatively straightforwardly, with a corresponding increase in productivity. More commonly, though, the potential team continues to muddle along without any particularly clear direction.

The **high-performance team**, according to Katzenbach and Smith, is the realization of the ultimate in team potential. High-performance teams have members who are deeply committed, not only to the team's success, but also to one another's personal growth and development – a relationship which has developed through the close interaction and shared responsibility of the team's activities. These teams have extremely high performance achievements and often, in organizational terms, achieve goals which appear at the outset to be impossible. Although the team itself may have a limited life – typically, once the task has been achieved, the team will dissolve – the close working relationships which emerge between team members continue to act as a positive factor throughout their subsequent organizational life.

Signs of high team performance

Evaluating where a team stands on the team performance curve can be simply a relatively straightforward matter of looking at the composition of the group, the range of skills and sense of common purpose which the group has, and whether it perceives group members as mutually accountable or not. But Katzenbach and Smith also identified a set of five distinctive signs that a group of people is really functioning as a team. These are: themes and identity, enthusiasm and energy, event-driven histories, personal commitment and, of course, performance results.

By themes and identity, Katzenbach and Smith are describing the way that a fully-developed team will have a number of recurrent ideas or patterns which, to the team members, express their basic purpose and the nature of the team itself. These themes may be expressed indirectly, as images, logos, mottoes or catchphrases, or they may be a patterned form of activity, like a regular gathering in the pub after work on Friday afternoon, where the team appraises the week's developments. Whatever they are, though, the meaning that the team derives from them, often unconsciously, is deeply symbolic of how the team members see their team.

Teams that are working well, Katzenbach and Smith argue, are also teams which are positive and energetic about their work. It is a deeply rooted aspect of human nature that we like to feel that our actions are effective; and working with others is equally deeply-rooted. A positively functioning team is therefore able to tap into deep levels of motivation, which manifest themselves in the energy that people put into their work, and in other signs like staying late to finish a task, voluntarily offering to help other team members and being enthusiastic about their tasks.

Another sign of positive team functioning, according to Katzenbach and Smith, is the way that a team evolves a history of its own. Events happen: setbacks, obstacles and difficulties; and as the team overcomes them, it also gains in strength and techniques. Each event contributes to a shared understanding within the team and to a greater awareness of the team's possibilities and potential. The anecdotes which emerge from them act as cautionary tales, or as inspirational stories which help to stimulate the team's performance.

Positive teams also develop a high degree of personal commitment between the team's members. The amount of shared experience which team members go through would probably be enough to establish this in itself, since working together so closely helps people to get to know one another very well. But in addition, this working together occurs in a positive atmosphere of achievement and of practicality; where weaknesses are not seen as a source of condemnation but as a signifier of a training need, and difficulties are met with co-operative and constructive suggestions.

The fifth, and vital sign of a positively functioning team identified by Katzenbach and Smith is that the team is achieving results. A real team, as they emphasize, is task-oriented: it is all about performance. And with that focus, together with the shared approach adopted by real and high-performance teams, it is almost inevitable that teams will out-perform working groups or sets of individuals engaged in similar tasks. The most distinctive feature of an effective team, always, is that it is producing specific, tangible results.

TEAM DECISION-MAKING

An entirely different aspect of evaluating team performance lies in the question of the way that teams make decisions. For many teams, decision-making is their primary function: management and executive teams, almost by definition, spend most of their time dealing with information and making decisions as a result. So do committees – and many public-sector organizations are run almost entirely by committees with different sectors of responsibility. So it is quite important that the team makes effective decisions. To evaluate this, we need to look at how they go about doing so – and whether they overcome the most serious pitfall of all – that of groupthink.

Group polarization

Interest in the area of group and team decision-making began to develop alongside the research into in how working groups operate, conducted during the 1960s and 1970s. At this time, there was a considerable amount of interest in white-collar groups and in particular, to the question of committee decision-making. Committees were becoming an increasingly large part of white-collar organizational life, so it was becoming increasingly necessary for managers and organizational consultants to understand something of the way that groups go about making decisions.

The issue was brought into sharp focus as a result of some research into risk in decision-making, conducted by Stoner in 1961, as part of a Master's Degree in Management. Popular assumption had it that groups would naturally tend to be conservative, opting for safe and cautious decisions. But Stoner showed that groups could actually make riskier decisions than individuals – the same people acting alone would be far more cautious than when they were acting as part of a decision-making group.

This phenomenon, which became known as **risky-shift**, adopted a great deal of interest – largely because of its dramatic implications for management practices. As research proceeded, however, it became apparent that the group's shift towards more risky decisions wasn't inevitable. Moscovici and Zavalloni (1969) showed that sometimes, groups would indeed make more cautious decisions than individuals, as had previously been thought.

What did seem to happen, though, was that making decisions in a group tended to exaggerate either the riskiness or the cautiousness of the decision. The direction would depend on how the group began its deliberations: if it was generally in favour of a cautious approach, then the ultimate decision would be more cautious than one taken by an individual; but if it was generally in favour of taking a chance, then the ultimate decision would be riskier. In other words, the decision became **polarized** – moving towards either the risky or the cautious end of the spectrum, but almost never towards the middle ground.

Given the advent of electronic mail systems and bulletin boards in the working environment, it is worth noting that another factor contributing to group polarization seems to be anonymity. Lea and Spears (1991) asked groups to communicate with one another using computers and compared the decisions that they made with groups who were interacting on a face-to-face basis. The computer-communicating group tended to make far more extreme decisions than the others.

Why does group polarization happen?
There are a number of possible explanations for why group polarization happens. One explanation is the idea that because the ultimate responsibility for the decision is shared by the whole group, people feel able to express themselves in a more extreme manner than they might if they were carrying the whole responsibility themselves: they are less individually accountable for its consequences. The computer experience might seem to offer some support for this idea. Another explanation is that people would vote for the option which looked most socially desirable. They would have learned this by discussing options, and becoming more aware of how other group members felt about the issue. And a third possibility is the one favoured by Moscovici and Zavalloni, who suggested that the group discussion provides people with more information than they would have had otherwise, so that they can get a clearer idea of why they are in favour of a cautious approach, or of a risky one.

As with most things that human beings do, group polarization is unlikely to have just one single cause. Instead, it is much more likely that each of these factors play some part in the phenomenon. It is an important phenomenon to know about when we are considering groups at work, however, since so many major organizational decisions are taken by committees of one kind or another.

Groupthink
Groupthink is an even more important aspect of group decision-making and one which can have very dramatic, and often disturbing, effects on an organization. It became recognized as a result of a book by Janis in 1972, which included a study of some extremely poor decisions made by high-level groups. Part of the work focused on decisions made by American Presidents, which later were shown to be serious blunders – such as Kennedy's decision to invade the Bay of Pigs in Cuba; or the decision to invade North Korea. Janis also looked at some disastrous business decisions, like the decision to market the drug Thalidomide and the Ford

Motor Company's decision to market the Edsel – one of the greatest failures in the history of mass-produced car manufacture.

Janis showed that these decisions were based on an entirely unrealistic perception of the situation, made in a committee environment in which more realistic information was never actually voiced. They generally happened when the group was isolated from outsiders and reasonably cohesive – a situation which is not at all uncommon in boardrooms. And groupthink was made even more extreme when there was a strong leader who was particularly keen on one course of action.

In many ways, long-term groups have a natural tendency towards assuming that the way they see the world is the only possible way, and that everyone else sees the world that way as well. We will be looking at another aspect of this when we look at organizations and social representations, in Chapter 6. It doesn't take much for this tendency to develop into groupthink – but, as we have seen, the consequences can be disastrous.

Symptoms of groupthink

There are a number of symptoms, though, which a group or team shows when it is suffering from groupthink. One of them is if the committee, board or task group operates under the illusion that it is largely **invulnerable** – a symptom which is easily detectable when we analyse recent financial disasters, such as the 1995 Barings Bank fiasco, in which the senior members of the bank failed to operate normal safeguarding procedures, and thereby allowed their Singapore trader to gamble away the bank's reserves on the stock exchange.

Another symptom is the committee's tendency to **rationalize** away unpopular solutions – to find justifications for not doing something which is necessary, but which wouldn't be particularly pleasant. A committee with a bad case of groupthink often falls back on **stereotyping** and deriding its opponents rather than arguing a case logically, and it will put considerable pressure on doubters among its membership to **conform**, rather than investigating the source of their doubts.

This pressure, or the expectation of it, also results in **self-censorship**: people on the committee, board or task group who have doubts about the wisdom of a decision will tend to keep quiet rather than speak up. This also can produce another symptom, which is an unrealistic impression of **unanimity** among the group members. Indeed, some people see unanimity as being the most telling symptom of all: if every member appears to agree with every decision then either someone, somewhere, is hiding their true opinions, or the group needs some new members who will bring a fresh point of view!

Another symptom of groupthink is that such groups often have members who act as '**mindguards**', by censoring undesirable information and opinions either directly, or by gentle hints, to those who come out with them that their behaviour isn't really acceptable. And an eighth symptom is that the group also operates under an 'illusion of **morality**' – they believe that their actions or decisions are intrinsically right and moral.

The effects of groupthink, as we've seen, can be extremely serious. Regrettably, despite our knowledge of the process, they still continue. A classic example was provided by Yorkshire Water in 1995, where the company's management had come to regard it as a business whose prime responsibility was to generate income for its shareholders and as a result had neglected long-term concerns about the water supply. Their failure to maintain and repair water supply systems adequately meant that a year which had begun with the area's reservoirs brim-full ended in serious water shortage and an expensive water-tankering operation which cost the company millions. Although by 1996 the company had come round to addressing the issue of leakage and repair more seriously, the power of the groupthink which had prevailed among its directors was apparent in their inability to acknowledge responsibility for the problem throughout most of the preceding year. Janis (1983) identified seven defects in decision-making which are likely to happen as a result of groupthink, which are listed in Table 5.3. Each of these was apparent in the Yorkshire Water case.

Box 5.2   Groupthink and the space shuttle disaster

Although knowledge about the dangers of groupthink and ways to avoid it has been widespread in management and psychological courses for many years now, that didn't stop it from affecting the NASA decision to launch the space shuttle Challenger in January 1986 – with tragic results. The temperature was well below the minimum temperature acceptable for safety and the shuttle exploded 73 seconds after launch, killing the seven people on board: six professional astronauts and one civilian, a schoolteacher. Moorhead, Ference, and Neck (1991) examined the details of that decision, which were gathered by the ensuing Presidential Commissions and found that every single one of the conditions for groupthink was present.

The three main antecedent conditions were present, in that the people who made the decision formed a cohesive group who had worked together for a long time. They had a strong leader preference for that particular decision, in the form of two top-level managers who actively promoted their opinions and other managers who pushed for launch; and they were also insulated from the experts who insisted that the launch was not safe, since the engineers gave their warnings early in the evening and were not allowed to participate in further discussion.

The eight symptoms were also present: the long history of freedom from accidents had produced an **illusion of invulnerability**, and the group also **rationalized** away the engineers' warnings by demanding absolute proof that the mission was unsafe. Absolute proof, of course, can never be achieved, but in any case the normal procedure was that it was necessary to be certain that it was safe, not that it was unsafe. The group also preserved its **illusion of morality** by refusing to acknowledge – and in some cases even notice – the strong ethical objections put forward by one high level manager and it dismissed the concerns of the engineers by **stereotyping** and dismissing them.

There was a considerable amount of **pressure on dissent** exerted by the top-level officials who supported the launch.

They pressurized representatives of Morton Thiokol (MTI) who had originally recommended that the launch should not take place and also put pressure on their personnel to prove that the launch was unsafe. This in turn produced **self-censorship**: for example, a Vice-President of MTI bowed to this pressure after some time and remained silent afterwards. This, as well as the silence from others following the example, produced an **illusion of unanimity** which was taken as support for the decision by those who were in favour of it. In addition, some members engaged in **mind-guarding** the group, by not revealing information which would have run counter to the group's expressed opinion.

The outcome, as might have been expected, was that the decision-making process showed all of the defects identified by Janis. The outcome was one of the worst disasters in space history and one which crippled the American space programme.

(Source: Moorhead, Ference and Neck 1991)

Cultivating dissent

As we saw earlier in this chapter, there are powerful social pressures on people to conform to group norms and to avoid confrontation. And when you add on issues about power and hierarchy, it becomes even more difficult. So it is all very well for a manager to say 'of course my staff can disagree with me', but it actually needs a bit more sensitivity than that. A committee chairperson or group leader who really wants to know what people think will need to try quite hard to create an atmosphere in which that can happen. It means showing, in practice, that dissent is welcomed and alternative views are taken seriously, which means suppressing the temptation to dismiss alternative ideas quickly.

That may not be as easy as it sounds, of course. It's very comfortable for managers to feel that people agree with them and dealing with dissent can often be awkward at first. It can also feel very threatening to the person who is being disagreed with. But having people in a team, committee or board of directors who can express an external view, or who have different perceptions

Table 5.3 Defects in decion-making arising from groupthink (source: Janis 1983)

1.	The alternatives to a given proposal are not fully explored
2.	The group doesn't examine its objectives in undertaking the action
3.	The group doesn't examine the risks involved in its choice
4.	The group doesn't reappraise alternatives which were rejected early on in the discussion
5.	The way that information is sought out by the group is poor and patchy
6.	The group is selective about which information it notices or deals with
7.	The group doesn't work out any contingency plans to deal with failure, if their choice doesn't work out

of what is happening and are not afraid to say so, can be absolutely vital.

According to Janis, the American President Kennedy actively cultivated dissent after the fiasco of the Bay of Pigs, with the fortunate result that by the time the Cuban Missile Crisis happened, he and his advisers were able to make far more sensible and realistic decisions and avert the crisis. Kennedy adopted a policy of deliberately encouraging confrontation, challenge and debate, and the result was a far more open and sensible form of decision-making. So it can be done. But given our psychological tendency to conform and to avoid confrontation, an atmosphere of dissent and debate is something which needs to be cultivated: it doesn't happen automatically.

Manz and Sims (1982) discussed how easy it is for self-managing work teams to slip into groupthink. There are two important factors in this: first, the fact that members of these teams interact with one another a great deal and gain significant amounts of support from one another. This raises the level of cohesiveness in the team, which in turn makes it vulnerable to groupthink. The second factor is to do with the way that the working team members depend on one another for completion of their tasks, which means that they are more likely to conform with one another's views than if they were working independently.

Teamthink

But groupthink isn't inevitable in these situations. Neck and Manz (1994) discussed how self-managing teams can oppose the pressures for groupthink and instead cultivate a different, more positive approach to decision-making, which the researchers called **teamthink**. The foundation of teamthink, Neck and Manz propose, is using positive cognitive strategies, of the sort which have been shown to result in more open decision-making and less of the narrow focus which is associated with threat and negative pressures. A great deal of evidence in many different areas of applied psychology shows that people can adopt different types of thinking strategies; and that optimistic, positive approaches tend to be more productive of ideas and to result in higher levels of achievement than ones which are pessimistic or negative. Neck and Manz propose that this can work just as well at the group level as it does with individuals.

Team leaders are very important in this, since they are able to set the tone of discussions and approaches within their teams, and to steer negative or pessimistic approaches into more positive channels. Teamthink, Neck and Manz suggest, is strongly influenced by the **beliefs** and **assumptions** which the team makes about why things happen and how they shape the way the team sees its choices. For example, one particularly negative belief strategy is to see things as if they were black-and-white alternatives, instead of recognizing that they are usually a bit more complex than that. Seeing things in arbitrary categories isn't usually very constructive – for instance, seeing someone simply as an 'enemy' may blind team members to occasions when that person may actually be prepared to support the team. Maintaining positive beliefs and assumptions helps to encourage a fuller exploration of alternatives and so helps the team to make better decisions.

There are other factors, too, which can help to encourage teamthink, such as cultivating what Bandura (1989) referred to as positive **self-efficacy beliefs**. These are the beliefs which we all hold about whether we are able to act effectively in particular situations: whether we expect ourselves to be able to do something or not. In self-managing teams, these are all to do with whether the team perceives itself as able to overcome challenges or not. Again, this is something where the tone set by the leader, and the way that the leader approaches difficulties, can be crucial. A team which sees itself as able to overcome challenges – even if it means learning new skills or developing new forms of influence – is a team which is able to respond positively to new ideas.

The outcome of this, and similar cognitive strategies which are cultivated by the team, is that instead of taking a restricted approach to decisions, in which just one choice is favoured and alternatives are not really taken seriously, the team develops much more constructive thought patterns. These lead it to encourage divergent views from team members; to develop an atmosphere where there is an open expression of concerns or ideas; where the team is actively aware of limitations or threats to the possibilities which it is considering; where it recognizes that its members are unique and have their own views, which may differ from one another; and in which collective doubts are aired and openly discussed rather than dismissed.

These, according to Neck and Manz (1994), are the characteristics of teamthink. Instead of the restricted, dysfunctional approach to decision-making produced by groupthink, teamthink produces a positive, dynamic and open approach, which allows the team to respond effectively to new and unforeseen situations. The two are quite different, yet a self-managing team can go in either direction. It will depend very much on the team's leader, the team's manager, and the team members themselves whether positive approaches are discussed and adopted; which is why awareness of groupthink and its alternatives is pretty important for successful team management.

REWARDS AND INCENTIVES

The issue of evaluating team performance leads naturally to the question of how teams should be rewarded. There has been a considerable amount of interest in the question of team rewards. Most organizations have reward systems which are based entirely on the appraisal of individuals. Yet the achievements of a well-performing team are synergistic: the contributions of each individual produces team achievements which are greater than, and different from, what could have been achieved by those individuals working alone. The question, therefore, is whether it would be more appropriate to reward the achievements of the team as a whole and whether it is divisive and counter-productive to continue to reward individuals alone.

Social loafing

One of the most important issues that we need to consider when we are looking at this question is the problem of **social loafing**. Social loafing is the psychological term for the way that some people, when they are working in a group, will actually put in **less** effort than they do when they are working alone. Latané *et al.* (1979), in discussing social loafing, defined it as 'a decrease in individual effort due to the social presence of other persons'. However, later research has shown that this is a little misleading, in that social loafing isn't only due to other people being present. There are some instances, for example, where people actually work harder when they are working with others. So it is important for successful team management that we are aware of what those circumstances are, in order that we can get the best out of the teamworking situation.

In part, as we can see from Box 5.3, the question of social loafing has everything to do with team size, and how recognizable each team member's efforts are. Harkins and Jackson (1985) showed how social loafing disappears completely in situations where people working in a group believe that their efforts or contributions will be observed and evaluated. But if this is not the case, and the individual's contribution to the group is simply merged anonymously with the whole group's achievements, then social loafing is much more likely to happen.

So one of the first messages for successful team management is that, even if a team reward system is introduced, there must also be some way of appraising and evaluating the contributions of the team members. It makes sense, really: after all, each of us likes to be appreciated. Rewarding individuals for their contributions to major achievements is a very effective way of enhancing their personal motivation.

Reward or punishment?

The question of whether it is better to use rewards for effective performance, or sanctions (punishments) for ineffective ones, is rather more tricky. Psychologists have known for a long time that rewarding appropriate behaviour is more useful than punishing inappropriate behaviour. Reward systems provide clear feedback to the person about what they should be doing and what is appreciated, whereas sanctions don't give any such message – if a person is genuinely at a loss as to how to do a task correctly, then

Box 5.3   **Teams, coaction and social loafing**

One of the recurrent bits of advice in the team management literature is that teams should be as small as they can possibly be and still get the job done. Don't have large teams, consultants argue: have small, streamlined teams where each member has different expertise and makes different contributions. This isn't just a matter of economizing: it also makes sound psychological sense. The reason why lies in the two psychological phenomena of coaction and social loafing.

Normally, when people are working with one another, or with other people around, they will work harder than they would do if they were alone. The principle of **coaction** was discovered back at the end of the last century, when it was observed that people would put more effort into a physical task if someone was working with them, than they would when they were working on their own (Triplett 1898). Having other people around usually spurs us on to greater efforts.

But it does depend on how many other people there are involved in the activity. If there are too many, so that the individuals involved are difficult to distinguish, then a different principle seems to come into play. This is the principle of **social loafing**: the observation that, under those circumstances, people actually put less effort into what they are doing than they would if they were working alone. In a large team, social loafing can become a significant problem. If nothing else, it can make the team less efficient than the same individuals would be if they were working independently.

Studies of social loafing have shown that one of the most important factors influencing it is whether, and to what extent, group members feel personally responsible for what is produced. In a group where the members are relatively anonymous, and each person's contribution is much the same as anyone else's, social loafing is quite likely – although it can be reduced by appropriate reward systems. But in a group in which everyone makes a different contribution, or where each person's contribution is apparent to everyone else, then coaction comes into play and people work harder.

So the management principle that the ideal size of a team is the minimum number to get the job done has sound psychological reasoning behind it. The biggest mistake in this area is to assemble a team by seeking to make it representative of the organization and choosing people from different departments purely to ensure that those departments are included. The way a team is assembled needs to be carefully worked out on the basis of what the team needs to do and whether a particular set of individuals has, or can develop, the skills and abilities that they need to do it.

punishing them for doing it badly won't be any help. In addition, punishment has been shown to be less effective because it complicates people's ability to work effectively by generating emotions such as anxieties, fear, resentment and even rebelliousness.

As I said, the difference in effectiveness between reward and punishment has been known for a great many years, and it is widely acknowledged in organizational and management circles. However, even though motivation through incentive and reward systems is the official policy of many organizations, that doesn't necessarily mean that rewards are used on a day to day basis. At a personal level, many managers are still more ready to use sanctions such as direct reprimands or sarcasm with their staff, than they are to say 'well done' or 'that's a good job, thank you'.

George (1995) conducted a study of how rewards and sanctions affected social loafing in a sample of 448 salesmen, who were working in groups of between four and ten members. Each of the salespeople was asked to complete questionnaires about their supervisor's behaviour and the types of rewards or sanctions which they encountered at work. Their supervisors were asked to complete her Social Loafing Scale (see Table 5.4) for each of the employees taking part in the study. George was particularly interested in the difference between whether the salespeople received generalized rewards or sanctions for their team's overall performance, or whether they received rewards or sanctions which were contingent on a particular individual's behaviour.

Table 5.4 The social loafing scale (source: George 1992)

Supervisors are instructed to rate each item for each employee, using the five-point scale:1 = not at all characteristic; 2 = slightly characteristic; 3 = somewhat characteristic; 4 =characteristic; 5 = very characteristic.

1.   Defers responsibilities he or she should assume to other salespeople.

2.   Puts forth less effort on the job when other salespeople are around to do the work.

3.   Does not do his or her share of the work.

4.   Spends less time helping customers if other salespeople are present to serve customers.

5.   Puts forth less effort than other members of his or her work-group.

6.   Avoids performing housekeeping tasks as much as possible.

7.   Leaves work for the next shift which he or she should really complete.

8.   Is less likely to approach a customer if another salesperson is available to do this.

9.   Takes it easy if other salespeople are around to do the work.

10.   Defers customer activities to other salespeople if they are present.

What George's research showed is that the most effective way of reducing social loafing is for the supervisor or manager to make sure that the rewards which the individual receives are ones which are directly linked to his or her own actions, rather than to the team's performance as a whole. Giving **contingent rewards** like this carries a lot of messages. It tells the person that their efforts have been noticed and are seen as valuable, as well as giving the person feedback about his or her own competence and effectiveness.

As we can see from Table 5.5, however, contingent sanctions don't have anything like the same effect. As Deci showed (e.g. Deci 1971), sanctions or punishments carry messages which range far beyond simple feedback about how the person has acted.

Table 5.5 Rewards, punishments and social loafing (source: George 1995)

	Contingent on individual acts or behaviour	Non-contingent on individual acts or behaviour
Reward	Decreases social loafing	No effect on social loafing
Punishment	No effect on social loafing	Increases social loafing

Contingent sanctions, one might think, would act to prevent social loafing because they would show the individual that their efforts were being noticed. Unfortunately, however, this effect is cancelled out by another, equally important one. Sanctions are really only possible when one person has direct power over the other. In a working context, using sanctions drives home the fact that the person is a subordinate and powerless: from the receiver's end, it comes across as organizational bullying. This generates resentment and means that punishment is just as likely to encourage social loafing – as a way of expressing that resentment – as it is to discourage it. As George showed, the net effect is that contingent sanctions don't appear to make any difference to social loafing.

Generalized rewards, which are not contingent on the individual team member's actions, might be expected to encourage social loafing too. After all, if you are likely to receive the reward whether you personally make an effort or not, then there would seem to be little point in trying particularly hard. But, as we can see, George's results showed that this was not the case: non-contingent rewards didn't influence social loafing one way or the other. The effect of encouraging social loafing seemed to be cancelled out by the need for the salespeople to produce a fair 'social exchange'. People prefer to reciprocate when they receive benefits or rewards – which is the explanation for the other well-known finding, that those who are slightly over-paid by comparison with others in similar employment work harder for their employers. So again the two mechanisms, one encouraging social loafing and the other discouraging it, cancel one another out producing no relationship between the two.

Generalized sanctions, on the other hand, were directly damaging. Penalizing a team or working group for low achievement without relating it to individual action increases social loafing significantly. One reason is that it is perceived by those individuals who have been making efforts as unfair: social exchange mechanisms which act to minimize social loafing are on the basis of a fair reciprocation: effort for reward. If effort is met with sanction, then the human response is to try to restore the balance and to stop trying. Sanctions which are not contingent on individual actions also generate negative emotions and resentment, which are likely to find expression in social loafing.

Team or individual reward?

The conclusions, then, are that in any teamworking system, the team members will need individual feedback and reward. Teamworking cannot be used as an excuse to omit personal recognition, since the contributions of the people who are working in the team make the team's success possible – and that needs to be acknowledged by the organization and by the team's manager. Individual recognition and reward strengthens personal motivation and makes sure that everybody contributes fully to the team. Sanctions, on the other hand, are best avoided as much as possible. They don't motivate people to work any harder and at their worst they can actively encourage social loafing.

But these findings do not mean that rewarding the team's efforts as a whole is entirely pointless. It may not make much difference to reducing social loafing, which always needs to be dealt with on individual terms. But it does make a great deal of difference to the team's sense of distinctiveness and membership, and it can help to reinforce bonds and shared experience between the team members. There is a strong case for rewarding team performance as a whole, in strengthening both the social identification between the team members, and also the relationship between the team as a whole and the parent organization that the team belongs to. Individual reward systems are necessary, but they are not enough on their own. The most effective systems of all are reward and incentive systems which operate at **both** individual and team levels.

SUMMARY

- Psychometric approaches to team measurement have included the Belbin Team Role Self-Perception Inventory and specialized scoring systems for the 16PF and OPQ. However, assessments of team role may not take account of more subtle aspects of team functioning.
- The Team Climate Inventory locates team functioning in its organizational context and looks at the relationship between organizational innovation and teamworking in terms of four dimensions: participative safety, support for innovation, vision and task orientation.
- Katzenbach and Smith proposed evaluating team performance by using themes and identity, enthusiasm and energy, event-driven

histories, personal commitment, and performance results to identify where a team would fall on their team performance curve.

- Research into the cognitive aspects of group decision-making highlighted two important mechanisms. One of these is group polarization, which is the tendency of groups to make more extreme
decisions than individuals would make if acting on their own.

- A second cognitive mechanism in group decision-making is
groupthink, which is the tendency for highly cohesive groups to
become self-centred and divorced from reality. This leads them to
make unrealistic and sometimes disastrous decisions, and is only
challenged by cultivating dissent.

- Self-managing teams can oppose groupthink by cultivating
teamthink, which involves positive thinking styles, and is particularly influenced by shared beliefs and assumptions and by the
self-efficacy beliefs held by team members.

- Team reward systems which do not also recognize individual
contributions can encourage social loafing. Sanctions have also
been shown (yet again) to be less effective than rewards in
encouraging positive contributions to teamworking.

Box 5.4 **Management recommendations**

Examine the psychometric adequacy of any checklists or
measuring instruments used to select or evaluate teams.
Use only those which have been carefully validated explicitly for use with teams.

Try appraising work teams using the five criteria of
themes and identity, enthusiasm and energy, event-driven
histories, personal commitment, and performance results.
Contrast these with your usual method of evaluation and
identify any benefits or insights which result from this exercise.

Cultivate open dissent and debate in meetings, and systematically encourage committee members to put forward
new perspectives and ideas, even if they seem impractical or
unwelcome at first.

Identify the reward and incentive systems operating on
team members. Ensure that they reflect individual effort and
attainment as well as the team's achievements as a whole.

6 *The team in its organization*

Teams don't exist in isolation. A working team is located in a larger organization and that organization exerts a considerable amount of influence on how the team is able to work. But a team can also influence the organization in which it is located. If we are to understand what leads to successful team management, we also need to understand how teams and their organizations interact with one another – which is what this chapter is all about.

HOW TEAMS INTERACT WITH THEIR ORGANIZATIONS

For many years, it was generally assumed that the most important factor in team performance was the internal group processes of the team itself – the team roles and team interaction which we have looked at in previous chapters. But this idea was challenged by the findings of a detailed study of 100 telecommunications sales teams, conducted by Gladstein (1984). Originally, the study was intended to focus purely on internal group processes, but from the very beginning the salesmen described how important their relationships were with other parts of the organization – particularly the repair and installation departments.

As a result, Gladstein modified the proposed survey to include questions about how the sales teams interacted with other groups in their organizations, expecting that they would show up as yet another aspect of the task which the team had to perform. But as the results emerged, it became apparent that Gladstein had tapped into a far more significant issue. The difference between internal and external activities was actually the most important distinction which people made when they were thinking about their team's activities. Although it had been almost overlooked by organizational researchers, the internal-external dimension turned out to be the main factor in team members' perceptions of their work.

Types of external activity

Following this insight into team processes, Ancona and Caldwell (1988) began a systematic investigation of the different ways that teams interact with their external environments. They began by conducting a series of interviews with managers of 38 new-product industrial teams, asking about many different features of the team's work and experiences, and linking this with other data obtained from daily records of external interaction and activities from records kept by each member of two of the teams in the study. This research project allowed them to identify a set of fifteen different activities by which teams interact with the outside world and these are described in Table 6.1.

Ancona and Caldwell found considerable variation between the teams in who undertook which activities. Some of these were

Table 6.1   External activities (source: Ancona and Caldwell 1988)

1.	Mapping
2.	Gathering information and resources
3.	Scanning
4.	Feedback-seeking
5.	Opening up communication channels
6.	Informing
7.	Co-ordinating
8.	Negotiating
9.	Moulding
10.	Allowing entry
11.	Translating
12.	Filtering
13.	Classifying
14.	Delivering
15.	Protecting

performed by most or all of the group members, while others might only be carried out by one person. Who did what, though, was much less important than whether it was done at all.

In 1990 the same researchers reported a further study, looking at how the various activities might be grouped together. They produced a questionnaire based on their list of activities and obtained responses from over 400 people, representing 45 industrial new-product teams. Their analysis revealed four major types of external activity, which they called 'ambassador', 'task co-ordinator', 'scout' and 'guard' activities. These types are listed and described in Table 6.2.

Having identified these types of external activity, the researchers then looked at how the three main ones related to what teams

Table 6.2   Types of external activity (source: Ancona and Caldwell 1990)

Ambassador	People undertaking this type of activity protect the team from outside pressure, persuade other people to support the team, represent the team to other members of the organization, particularly those in influential positions, and lobby for resources.
Task co-ordinator	This type of activity includes discussing design problems with other people, negotiating manufacturing and production requirements, obtaining feedback on the product and discussing marketing strategies and supply implementation with the relevant departments.
Scout	This type of activity is concerned with gathering general information about the outside environment, such as new product developments, changes in the proposed market, or technical standards. It includes exploring alternative ideas and possibilities for new markets, the acquisition of detailed market information and the monitoring of competitor activities.
Guard	Unlike other activities, this type of activity is primarily about ensuring that information doesn't pass from the team to the outside. It includes keeping news about the team secret from the rest of the company, protecting the product by maintaining absolute secrecy about it within the organization, and controlling the release of information from the team in order to make sure that the 'appropriate' picture is presented to the rest of the organization.

actually did when they were working. Some teams, which they described as 'ambassadorial', tended to focus their external activities on ambassadorial activities and little else. 'Technical scouting' teams engaged in a combination of task co-ordination and scout activities. 'Isolationist' teams didn't really do much in the way of outside-oriented activities at all, apart from a minimal amount of scout activity; while 'comprehensive' teams combined ambassadorial and task co-ordination, but did relatively little scouting. A new set of investigations, with an entirely new sample of new-product teams (Ancona and Caldwell 1992), showed that there were considerable differences in how effectively these teams carried out their tasks.

What do successful teams do?

What emerged most clearly of all from Ancona and Caldwell's research was that each of the successful teams engaged in a great deal of **ambassadorial activity**. Some of the most successful had begun this activity even before the team had really been established. The team leaders took that as one of their most important responsibilities and they continued it throughout the life of the project. Perhaps not surprisingly, ambassadorial activities were also considered by high-level managers to be the most important team activity of all. In one case, an 'ambassador' was added to a team by the management half-way through the project, because the team leader had avoided this activity.

Teams with a high level of **task co-ordinator activities** also tended to be successful. Linking with manufacturing to ensure that their product design could be implemented, gathering information from sales and other departments about what was practical and what wasn't, ensuring that the necessary resources would be available when particular phases of the project were reached – these were typical task co-ordinator activities and were all activities which were considered essential to a team's success. This was such an important point that in one of the teams a leader who didn't engage in any of these activities was actually demoted and a team leader from the manufacturing side of the company was put in his place. (This, incidentally, was the same team who had had an 'ambassador' added to their number as a 'resource' earlier on). The two new members encouraged other members of the team to make their own external contacts instead of passing everything through the team leader. Gradually, as a result of their efforts, the project team became revitalized and, in the end, successful.

Interestingly, though, Ancona and Caldwell's research showed that **scouting** activities didn't particularly link with team success – indeed, they found that those teams which engaged in a great deal of scouting were actually *less* likely to be successful than those which didn't. It seems that a certain amount of scouting activity at the beginning of the project can be useful, to ensure that the teams are on the right track. Once work has begun in earnest, though, scouting becomes counter-productive because it keeps throwing new ideas and possibilities at the team, instead of letting them get down to work seriously with the design or option which they have selected.

One team which Ancona and Caldwell investigated never, in fact, got any further than scouting even after nine months, because the product which they had been set up to investigate had so many possibilities that they had been unable to fix on just one and get on with it. Their team leader avoided top management and no one else engaged in either ambassadorial or task co-ordination activities. Eventually, despite a very supportive initial start from the parent organization, the project had to be killed off.

We can see, then, that the way that a team interacts with its organization can make a great deal of difference to its overall success. The research done by Ancona and Caldwell dealt primarily with new product design teams, so it may not be typical of all types. But it did show how their work, although on the surface simply a matter for the team itself, actually depends very strongly on the type of external liaison and interaction in which the team engages.

Other types of teams, too, work in a wider organizational context and often need the support of other departments or groups if they are to be able to innovate, or even carry out routine jobs well. And even apparently isolated teams, such as those running an older person's home, can benefit greatly from a supportive organization and community. To a large extent, it will be the team's own external activity which influences how supportive the outside organization is likely to be.

Characteristics of supportive organizations

In 1980, Thomsett argued that what is important for a team within an organization is whether the organization has a supportive

Box 6.1   **The employee as ambassador**

Ambassadorial activity doesn't have to be confined to nominated individuals. A whole team, or even a whole company, can become involved in promoting the interests of the organization, representing it positively and persuading other people to support it. Moreover, if the organization provides scope for its staff to be proud of belonging to it, employees will often embrace these activities wholeheartedly.

I saw a clear example of this in a small computer company, 'DataWork', which I visited on a consultancy basis from time to time. The company had grown to about 40 staff when the managing director decided to devote some attention to the interface between the company staff and the customer. In conventional terms, of course, it was only the sales staff and the receptionist who were actually expected to deal with customers. The technical staff who made up the majority of the employees were engaged in 'back-room' software development work and at the most were only expected to deal with exceptional computer problems which customers might experience.

None the less, the managing director decided to invest a full day of company time on a sales awareness course. An outside trainer who specialized in this area was brought in and all of the company's personnel were expected to attend. When I visited the company a few weeks later, the staff were still buzzing with the lessons which they had learned. Even those who would not normally have expected to deal with customers felt more confident that they could do so when it was required of them and all of them had learned to treat even the smallest contact with outsiders as manifestations of their responsibilities as ambassadors for the company.

The managing director's decision to invest that amount of employee time – which was considerable for a company of that size – was a shrewd one. By involving all of the staff, he had managed to generate a shared experience and set of values which formed the basis for a great deal of future discussion and interaction. By communicating to his staff that each person was important enough to warrant this

training, he had managed to generate a sense of responsibility and involvement, and also a sense of directly contributing to the company's success. And by emphasizing the
company's external image in this way, he had ensured that
all of his employees felt confident and empowered to represent the company should the need arise. When the company
reorganized its work a few months later, giving particular
techical staff responsibility for particular clients, his people
were trained and ready.

culture – a culture which will help and encourage the team to
function in the best way possible. Thomsett identified a number of
important features of supportive cultures in organizations. One of
these is that there should be a general belief in the organization
that the people in the organization are an asset to be developed,
rather than just rigid performers of tasks. Another is that the staff
should be grouped in an enlightened fashion, so that people who
have skills and expertise work together in appropriate groups,
rather than working in scattered isolation throughout the organization. Moreover, people's skills should match the roles which
they are expected to play and natural groups should be allowed to
form.

An organization which has a participative management structure and a flat management shape, as opposed to a management
structure with layer upon hierarchical layer, will enhance effective
teamwork. So too will a control system which emphasizes self-
regulation, instead of one which applies external controls like
close supervision and excessive cross-checking procedures. These
organizations, in Thomsett's view, also tend to have a high level
of commitment among their members, with people tending to
collaborate rather than compete with one another in a congenial
environment which encourages co-operation to happen.

A hostile environment, on the other hand, can make it extremely
difficult for a team to function effectively. Kanter (1983) pointed
out how trying to operate in an atmosphere of threat and anxiety –
fear of cutbacks, redundancy and down-sizing – works against
effective teamwork. This happens mainly because the emotional
background of fear and anxiety begins to influence managerial

policies, which become defensive and mistrustful. That sort of climate prevents effective teamwork because teams need to be allowed to operate with a certain amount of autonomy; and also with a certain amount of confidence that their membership will stay reasonably consistent for a period of time. That autonomy requires trust from the management and consistency can't be expected if staff are working in an atmosphere of redundancy threats.

Organizational cultures

Research into team activities and the characteristics of supportive organizations all points to the idea that the **organizational culture** within which the team is operating is a vital factor in how well the team is able to function. For this reason, it is worth taking a fairly thorough look at what we mean by the term organizational cultures, how cultures manifest themselves in different organizations and how they influence the people who work in them.

All through the twentieth century, organizational researchers studied highly successful companies, trying to identify management practices which could help to improve the performance of less successful companies. Their research showed that large, successful organizations, such as IBM, had consistent 'styles' of interpersonal interaction and of management, which permeated the whole organization. These companies also tended to perform consistently well in the market-place. The idea that some styles of management were likely to be more successful than others took a firm hold. By the 1980s, it had become particularly important to understand this, as so many large and small firms failed to adapt to changing economic climates, while others appeared to cope relatively easily.

International competition played its part in clarifying the concept. The economic success shown by Japanese firms prompted many organizational researchers to look closely at how these firms operated. Studies of Japanese systems of management showed vast differences in the approaches, beliefs and assumptions permeating the whole company, and in the way that these were maintained by the leadership. In many ways, this fitted with the findings from studies of high-performing Western organizations, which had also suggested that central values and overarching beliefs were typical of those organizations. These comparisons

focused attention on the metaphor of organizations as being min-
iature societies – cultures – in their own right.

Cultures as types

As the idea of organizational cultures became more sophisticated,
several different kinds of theory emerged. One of them, which
appealed to many because it seemed to provide a straightforward,
simple account, was the idea that there were just so many different
types of culture. For example, Harrison (1972), developed a rather
simplistic **typology** in which organizational cultures were divided
into four types: (i) power cultures, typified by centralized control
and rapid action (ii) role cultures, typified by strictly defined
administrative procedures (iii) task cultures, typified by a dominating concern with getting the job done (iv) person cultures,
typified by a concern for employee welfare and progress. Each of
these types is supposed to be associated with distinctive organizational structures.

This way of looking at an organization, of course, doesn't take
account of teams or teamworking. But in real life, plausible though
this model may be, it doesn't really work. Organizations, like
people, just aren't that simple. A real-life organization is likely
to have some of the characteristics of one culture and some of the
characteristics of another. Classifying organizations into rigid
categories means that we have to ignore most of the features which
make that organization special and yet often, it is those special
characteristics which make an organization's culture distinctive.

Another problem is that organizations are not the same all the
way through. Harrison's typology, and others like it, present a
vision of a consistent universe in which organizations have just
one culture, shared by staff who know their place and interact
consistently and logically. But again, real life just isn't like that.
Organisations consist of departments, sections, networks, groups
and teams and each of those can develop their own consistent
styles and approaches. What is taken for granted in the boardroom
can be regarded as very unlikely on the shop floor and irrelevant in
the finance department. So describing organizations as if they are
the same all through is a little bit dubious. But using these
differences positively through adopting a teamworking philosophy
can, oddly enough, help to bring consistency into an organization's culture.

Cultures as symbols

A different approach to organizational culture involved looking at the symbols and patterns which held the organization together. Both the highly successful Western companies, such as IBM and Mars and the equally highly successful Japanese companies like Honda and Sony, adopted distinctive symbols and slogans which represented the company, and which ran throughout just about every aspect of working life. Organizational symbolism can take many forms: rites, rituals and customs; metaphors and slogans; myths and organizational legends; or artefacts like logos, architecture or design. The management guru Tom Peters, in an influential article, even argued that the manipulation and conscious use of organizational symbols could provide the key to changing organizational cultures successfully (Peters 1978) – although nowadays, we recognize (as does Peters) that things aren't quite that simple.

Other researchers, too, discussed the various types of symbols in organizations and this **semiotic** approach to organizational culture became extremely popular. In many ways, it reflects a perceived need for establishing distinctiveness among members of the organization. The shared symbols help each member of the organization to see themselves as having something in common and as being distinctive from the outside world. In teamworking, it is sometimes useful for teams to have a rapid, distinctive way of expressing membership or summarizing a philosophy. But as a way of establishing a 'quick-fix' cultural change it is distinctly limited – largely because, as the other theorists realized, organizational symbols are signs of something deeper: they are not an end in themselves.

Cultures as systems

A third approach accepted the idea that organizational symbolism was an important feature of culture, but used it in a more interactive way. These researchers saw the symbols as expressing an underlying general **system** – a pattern of interaction and negotiation occurring between the people working in the organization and the organization itself. So they also studied other aspects of organizational functioning, such as how decisions were made, how influence and power operated within the organization, and who interacted with whom.

Systems analysis allowed researchers to develop guidelines or principles of how companies should be managed. Perhaps the clearest examples of these guidelines were outlined by Peters and Waterman (1982) in their book *In Search of Excellence*. These researchers identified eight principles as being the foundations for producing 'excellent' organizations – that is, organizations in both the public and private sectors which were high-performing, efficient and effective. The principles are listed in Table 6.3, but it is worth looking at them in more detail here.

The first principle is **a bias for action**, in that people in the organization are concerned with actually getting things done, rather than absorbing their time with paperwork and committees. Teams, task forces and small focused working groups are common; experimentation and learning experiences are frequent.

The second principle is that successful organizations are **close to the customer**. Everyone in the organization is fully committed to making sure that the customer's needs are satisfied. This produces an obsession with quality as well as with efficiency. The organizations also value and seek opinions and feedback from their customers.

Autonomy and entrepreneurship is the third principle of successful organizations outlined by Peters and Waterman. The organization encourages flexibility and dynamism among its work-force. Those responsible for successful initiatives are acknowledged as 'champions' and managers and teams are given the autonomy to explore new avenues and ideas. An important factor here is that the organization has a substantial tolerance for failure.

Table 6.3 Principles of excellent companies (source: Peters and Waterman 1982)

1.	A bias for action
2.	Close to the customer
3.	Autonomy and entrepreneurship
4.	Productivity through people
5.	Hands-on, value-driven
6.	Stick to the knitting
7.	Simple form, lean staff
8.	Simultaneous loose-tight properties

The fourth principle is **productivity through people**. In these organizations, the policy is to demonstrate respect for employees through training systems, providing clear and open information and discussing new initiatives. Employees are taken care of, appropriately trained and encouraged to develop. Special contributions from people at all levels in the organization are encouraged and acknowledged.

The fifth principle is that successful organizations are **hands-on, value-driven**. What the reseachers meant by this is that the best companies have a clear idea of what their company stands for – what its values are and the principles and policies which stem from those values. These values are shared with, and by, their staff and are taken very seriously as the special feature of the organization, which distinguishes it from the competition.

Peters and Waterman also advised successful organizations to **stick to the knitting**. Organizations which diversify too widely can lose their perspectives and, more importantly, their values. Unchannelled diversification is almost always a losing proposition for an organization. When management and employees have built up standards of excellence in their field, translating them to other areas of work always presents difficulties and generally results in a dilution of quality all round. Organizations need to recognize what they are good at and expand in those directions rather than into different ventures.

The seventh principle for successful organizations is **simple form, lean staff**. The more elaborate the chains of command, the more the inertia at the lower levels and the greater the risk that staff will become alienated from the main company values. The most dynamic organizations, Peters and Waterman argued, have a simple structural form with few levels of hierarchy. Since such a form results in greater involvement and autonomy from employees, this approach also means that fewer administrative and support staff are required to keep things running.

The eighth principle of successful organizations is that they have **simultaneous loose-tight properties.** Excellent organizations typically combine a firm, though streamlined, structure with a systematic encouragement of innovation and dynamism by providing the maximum individual autonomy to employees. The combination of firm principle and values with maximum employee involvement means that the organization gets the best of both worlds: it retains coherence and direction, but also retains enthusiasm, experimentation and entrepreneurship among its work-force.

Taken together, these eight principles add up to a model of organizational culture which emphasizes the systems and principles operating within the organization. The eight principles, extracted from the successful organizations of their time, offered a systematic approach to understanding how those organizations had achieved some of their successes. Although the model did attract criticism later – mainly because some of the successful organizations which Peters and Waterman had described did not make it through the recession of the late 1980s – it none the less provided a useful set of basic guidelines for company directors and high-level managers.

Cultures as shared beliefs

Schein (1985) argued that organizational culture actually goes deeper than either systems or semiotic approaches had assumed. Although organizational culture does, of course, incorporate symbols and systems, Schein asserted that the main core of any organizational culture is really a set of deeply-held shared beliefs and assumptions, which underpin everything that goes on. Distinctive organizations such as Mars don't just have organizational symbols. They also have characteristic and important beliefs about their employees and about how the world works. These underlying assumptions direct the approaches taken by managers and directors of the organization.

This idea, also, gradually became adopted by organizational researchers until, by 1990, Lundberg was able to describe a general consensus among researchers in the understanding of organizational culture. The new model presents organizational culture as operating on three levels. On the surface is the manifest level, which people come across when they visit or join the organization: the symbols, anecdotes and so on. It consists of symbolic artefacts, language, stories, ritualistic activities and various types of patterned conduct which happen in organizations.

Next comes the strategic level, which is about distinctive styles and approaches which people in the organization are likely to take. It consists of beliefs held by directors and managers about strategic vision and planning, capital/market expectations;

product/market competition; and internal systems. And underlying all of this is the core level, which consists of ideologies, values, assumptions and deeply-held beliefs. Essentially, it is a set of fundamental beliefs, about human nature, the world and what work is all about. It is this fundamental level which links the whole organizational culture together and gives it cultural unity.

Cultures as networks

Although it was a great deal more useful than seeing organizational cultures as simple 'types', even the layered approach to organizational culture still tended to assume that information and ideas would flow consistently through the organization from top management, and be adopted by all of the work-force without question. But, as we have already seen, most organizations aren't really that straightforward. Employees may be sceptical about new approaches; a department may have developed its own style over many years and resist changing it; middle managers may interpret information from the top in their own individual ways. The result, as Van Maanen and Barley (1985) pointed out, can become extremely fragmented.

These researchers proposed that it was probably more useful to see organizational cultures as networks of smaller groupings within the organization. Each department, division, team and working group would develop its own style and way of interacting. In some companies, these styles would overlap quite a lot, so that the approach taken by one department would be fairly similar to that taken by the others. Those are the organizations which we would describe as having 'strong' organizational cultures. In other organizations, though, there would be much less consistency between departments and their organizational culture would be much weaker (see Figure 6.1).

We can see, then, that (apart from the type theories) each new insight into organizational cultures has been able to link with previous ones, to enrich our understanding of why organizations are like they are. When we are looking at successful team management, some of these insights are more helpful than others. For instance, the idea of cultures as networks can help us to understand a great deal about how a team fits in with its organization, while the idea of a fundamental level of shared beliefs helps us to

A 'weak' culture organization

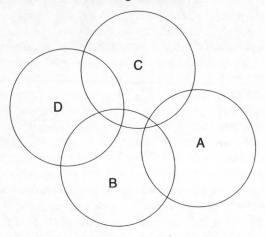

A 'strong' culture organization

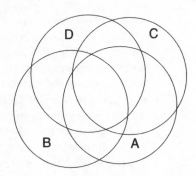

A,B,C and D represent departments within the organization. Strong
cultures show considerable overlap in beliefs and values; weaker ones
show litle overlap between departments

Figure 6.1   Strong and weak organizational cultures.

understand why developing shared values is such an important part of team-building.

SOCIAL IDENTITY AND THE ORGANIZATION

When we take the idea of cultures as networks, linking together the different groups within an organization, we can begin to understand why shifting to a team-based approach can be so useful to the organization as a whole and also why it can so often result in a major culture change. The process of social identification, which we have looked at so frequently in this book, shows how feeling that one is part of and belonging to a particular team helps people to contribute fully and effectively, and creates a climate which helps to maximize both team and individual performance. The same is true of social identification with a particular company or organization.

As I've remarked before, we all have a great many social identities – a great many groups to which we belong and with which we identify. I may, at different times, manifest a social identification as a family member, as a psychologist, as an organizational consultant, as a writer, or with a host of other groups. Some of our social identities, too, nest within others. As Ashforth and Mael (1989) pointed out, a person working in an organization can identify with their immediate working group, with their department, with their professional category and with the company as a whole; and none of these are necessarily in conflict. So another way in which an understanding of social identification can help successful team management is by making clear some of the ways that teams and other organizational groups interact with one another, within the same organization.

The social identity mechanisms which we have looked at through this book show us that it is basic to human beings to see the world in terms of in-groups and out-groups. It is this which makes teamworking such a very powerful organizational strategy. It gives people a clear sense of belonging to something special, while still fostering a sense of belonging to, and taking part in, the wider organization.

Avoiding intergroup hostility

Encouraging a distinctive sense of identity in the team is something which needs to be managed carefully, to make sure that the team doesn't come to see itself as totally different from, and in opposition to, others in the organization. People can easily exaggerate how different one group, team or department is from another and this can mean that they end up ignoring what they have in common and finding it hard to co-operate. Equally, though, it is possible for different groups to co-exist happily, co-operate with one another and work together towards mutual higher-order goals.

The secret of managing teams in such a way as to make sure that they retain their ability to co-operate with one another is to make sure that any competition is a matter of competing for achievement, but not for resources. As we've seen before, competition for resources is extremely damaging for any sense of unity within an organization. Although some top managers perceive it as 'healthy competition', it is usually distinctly unhealthy. For instance, it results in people spending far too much of their time and effort in protective or defensive activity and this is time which detracts them from their main work. It damages communication, since people belonging to one group are unwilling to let anyone in the other group know anything which they might turn to their advantage – and in a complex organization, that can be just about any type of information at all. It encourages political manoeuvering and lobbying. And at its most extreme, staff can become anxious, paranoid and unwilling to listen to anything which doesn't come from members of their own group. Apart from being a great waste of emotional energy, that contributes considerably to both organizational and individual stress.

Competition for resources, therefore, is a dangerous game. If we examine research into the effective, well-run team-centred organizations (which are not as rare as one might imagine) we find that almost without exception their various work teams share a common perception – of everyone working together towards shared, overarching goals and of each team contributing its bit towards the whole success of the organization.

That doesn't mean that competition has no place in teamwork. It does. But the competition involved in successful, teamwork-based organizations is to do with achievement, not resources. Teams can compete for recognition, awards and other things which signal how valuable their contribution to the organization has been. That type of competition is perfectly healthy and stimulates the development of an achievement-oriented culture in the organization as a whole. Competition for resources, on the other hand, simply encourages internal backbiting and resentment.

Team-building in the organization

A management approach which will allow a team to operate positively within its organization as a whole also needs to encourage a general sense of cohesion and identification throughout the work-force. There is no harm in each team having a distinctive identity – indeed, as we have seen, this can be very helpful – but that identity needs to be firmly located within the organization as a whole.

Avoiding intergroup conflict is one way of contributing to this, but there are also positive factors which can contribute to it. One example, for instance, is in social events. Many firms use regular informal get-togethers for their employees to help develop a sense of shared identity and teamwork – the Friday afternoon 'beer bash' which has become so common in high-tech computer organizations is a classic example. These events help people to work together and feel that they belong to the same organization. They foster shared memories of organizational events and the development of shared histories of the organization; stories about organizational heroes; and various anecdotes about managers and employees. All of which enrich the organization's culture and strengthen the common understanding of the people working in it.

Social events can be very helpful, but what is even more important in building organizational cohesion is internal communication: promoting the idea of membership of the group, through an understanding of the group – and the outside organization – as a functioning unit. This is not a new principle: one of the early Hawthorne studies featured a particularly effective informal leader who took new members around the factory so they could see where their own work fitted into the making of the final product. That particular department had a much lower apparent sense of alienation among its work-force and more importantly, in managerial terms, a lower rate of staff turnover than the other departments

Box 6.2 **Staff Turnover**

A high turnover of staff is a key symptom indicating that all is not well with an organization's management. If people feel demoralized or unappreciated, or if they see themselves as mistreated or underpaid, their first reaction is to seek another job. Typically, those who are the most competent and/or dynamic find it relatively easy to get another position and so leave the organization relatively quickly. Over time, this can mean that the organization is left with second-rate staff or those who, for one reason or another, feel trapped.

It is too easy, though, for managers to disregard the symptom of high turnover. The management of an office supply firm which I visited as a consultant mentioned the company's high rate of turnover as a constant source of problems. However, the reasons which the management gave for why staff left were always personal ones – so-and-so had marital difficulties; so-and-so was extremely ambitious and so on. It had never crossed their minds that their management style might have something to do with it.

As I interviewed the employees, I found that they made very different attributions about why people left. They saw it as a direct result of an excessively authoritarian, unappreciative management style, which provided no opportunities for training or self-development and which paid its people poorly. Although the employees had very helpful suggestions to make about how the organization could be run, they were never consulted by the management and many of the directives that they were given did not, actually, help them to do their work. In short, anyone who wanted job satisfaction or a proper career, the employees told me, simply had to leave: there was no future for them there. As I investigated the company further, it became apparent that this was no exaggeration.

This problem doesn't just apply to people working at lower levels in the organization. Gaertner and Nollen (1992) explored issues of leaving among top executives. By distinguishing between the desire to leave and the intention to leave, they found that it was possible to distinguish four categories: 'stayers', who wanted to remain with the organization and intended to do so; 'leavers', who wanted to leave and intended to do so; 'locked-ins', who believed that they would stay with the firm even though they didn't particularly want to; and 'jilteds', who wanted to stay with the firm but intended to leave none the less. People in the last category were those who felt, for one reason or another, that there was no future for them in the organization. Even though they were good at their jobs, they had been passed over for promotion, or what they were doing was failing to get recognition for one reason or another.

Fostering social identification through teamwork is one way of preventing such a strong sense of alienation from developing in the organization. People derive job satisfaction from belonging to a team with real responsibilities; and the process of empowering such a team so that it can work effectively also allows team members to develop by acquiring new skills and through training. Most of all, it gives people new challenges and a reason to feel proud of themselves and their team.

where the work was treated as self-contained and independent of the rest of the firm.

Effective communication helps team members to develop a sense of being part of the organization as a whole and also helps them to acknowledge the value of what different teams within the organization can contribute to their own team's success. Inadequate internal communication often results in failure to appreciate the contributions of others; and that can easily produce counter-productive resentments which interfere with organizational functioning. Making sure that everyone has a clear understanding of the role that each team plays in the organization helps to promote a positive sense of identification with the organization and the sense of working together towards shared goals.

ORGANIZATIONAL CULTURES AND SOCIAL REPRESENTATIONS

In Chapter 1 we looked at social representation theory, which is all about the shared beliefs which are held by groups and cultures. These shared beliefs take the form of mini-theories about what the world is like, about human nature and about how and why things do or do not change. They are used to justify social action (or inaction) and to explain why things happen the way that they do. More importantly, they often consist of implicit, taken-for-granted knowledge and people who hold particular social representations tend to assume that other people will automatically think in the same sort of way.

Social representation theory helps us to understand Schein's argument that underlying shared beliefs and assumptions are the distinctive features of organizational cultures. In a lot of ways, organizational cultures **are** social representations – they are ways of representing the realities of organizational life, which are negotiated and shared by individuals and working groups. They also encapsulate what people see as the most fundamental values and assumptions in the organization and express these, as social representations are expressed, through metaphor, anecdotes and symbols.

Seeing organizational cultures in this way also helps us to understand Van Maanen and Barley's model of cultures as interlocking groups. Organizational social representations can be large-scale, expressing beliefs held widely across the whole organization; or they can be smaller-scale, expressing beliefs which are only held by particular departments, working groups or teams. When the shared beliefs and assumptions held by working groups are similar across the organization, the organization has what we would call a strong culture; when they are very different from one another, it doesn't.

Sometimes, too, the social representations held by some groups in an organization are so different that they effectively form a counter-culture, directly challenging the aims and goals of the management (Davis 1985). These counter-cultures can be extremely resistant to organizational change and may result in the determined blocking of a new system or way of working which management is trying to introduce. In an organization which is trying to change in order to survive in a competitive market, that can be disastrous. It is here that getting positive working teams together, bringing together expertise from various departments and establishing new contacts between individuals can be a very strong asset.

Not all resistance to change is negative, though. Sometimes, it is really an attempt by those involved in the day to day work of the organization to preserve what the organization itself expresses as fundamental and important values. The clearest examples of this in recent years have come in the health services, when a patient care team committed to promoting patient health and ensuring high-quality treatment comes up against short-term management policies aiming to cut costs and lower services. To expect those who are actively working with patients to adopt policies which mean that their patients are likely to suffer is clearly unrealistic and often contrary to the organization's own avowed goals about the quality of patient care. As Anderson and King discuss in their book *Innovation and Change in Organisations* (ITBP 1995), this type of resistance to change may actually have a positive effect on the organization in the long term, since it may force the management to reappraise the situation.

What organizational culture theory shows us, then, is that it is the 'them-and us' groups which form the real working experience for the organization's staff. Whether people are perceived as being 'on our side' or not has a tremendous effect on how well employees work together. Organizational culture theory also shows us that it is possible to create a working environment in which the working groups which make up the organization act coherently together, without rivalry, to create a dynamic, positive atmosphere which pervades the whole organization. The policies and strategies of top management make it possible, but the 'glue' which holds it all together is the working relationships between the different groups. Teams, by providing a way that people with different skills come together to achieve a common goal, are a particularly effective way of unifying an organization's culture.

This discussion of organizational cultures may have seemed like a bit of a digression, but it isn't really. It makes it clear just how important teams can be to the organization as a whole. Organizations aren't just simple, unified structures: they consist of whole networks of different groups, with their own ways of working and their own belief patterns. Teams are a part of that and a part which has distinctive potential. That potential is partly because a well-functioning team is open to new ideas and new experiences. As we are about to see, teams can be a particularly potent force when we are looking to influence or change an organization's culture.

TEAMS AND ORGANIZATIONAL CHANGE

One of the most important tasks of the modern organization is coping with, and adapting to, change. The business environment is constantly changing and so is the environment in which public sector organizations operate. The mixture of greater competition, greater demand for high quality services and greater need for streamlined efficiency means that an organization which doesn't change ultimately becomes slow and unwieldy, easily outmanoeuvred by competitors and unable to operate effectively in a contemporary economic or social climate.

Teams have a great deal to contribute to organizational change. As we have already seen, an active, well-functioning team tends to be very clear about its own goals and values and also has good contacts with the rest of the organization. This helps the team to do its own job, of course, but it also has a useful by-product. It means that, because they have already been involved in exploring these issues, the team members are more likely to understand the characteristics of the organization, identifying clearly the factors which underlie or influence managerial policy. This helps them to spell out the reasons for change to working colleagues or other people. Teams which operate in this way can also have a valuable input into the formulation of the policy in the first place, if they are consulted by senior management.

Because team members have learned how to act in a coherent and directed fashion, teams can be a vital force in actually implementing organizational change. Working teams are in a position to receive, and be trained in, new styles of working and they can disseminate these new approaches to the rest of the organization. Organizational change almost always produces a certain amount of resistance and although, as we have seen, that resistance can sometimes be a matter of actually preserving important organizational values, it can equally well simply reflect inertia, with people preferring to carry on working in the way that they have always done. But dynamic working teams, as we have seen, tend to be task-oriented and the people in them have already adjusted to a different way of working. So they tend to be receptive to new approaches, or at least prepared to evaluate them thoroughly before rejecting them.

Many large-scale organizations have used team structure as the way of overcoming organizational inertia. By giving people the opportunity to experience different ways of working, they are able to show that the new ways can be advantageous and also that they they can be practical too (Katzenbach and Smith 1993). It is possible to use teamworking to give people a 'taste' of what new approaches might actually mean and to encourage people to focus on organizational goals and achievements. And, of course, by introducing new practices in this way, the teams are able to evaluate the changes and to let management know if – and how – they need to be modified.

How does organizational change happen?

Katzenbach and Smith (1993) argue that teams are more-or-less vital if an organization is facing major change. Without the impact of committed teams, able to range across the levels of the organization and to get over the message that 'change is necessary and here is one way to carry it out', nothing would actually happen. Trying to change organizations by working with individuals simply can't be as effective, they argue, because individuals on their own are so much less influential than groups of people who are all giving the same message. Teams are important for shaping the vision of organizational change, but they are equally important for spreading that change and carrying it out.

Moreover, Katzenbach and Smith believe that an organization which is based on effective working teams is one which is far more open to change, and which can respond better to its challenges than an organization which is based on traditional hierarchical authority. Because people are actively involved in their teams and because the team structure allows them to have a real say in how their work is carried out, they are more likely to make suggestions to improve their work and – just as impor-

Box 6.3   **Implementing organizational change**

In recent years, change has affected every kind of organization, including those which never anticipated any need for it. A particular case of this occurred in the 'Oldtown' local government payroll department, whose employees had not considered the need for change, on the grounds that local government staff would always need paying and that the payroll department was therefore secure.

A consequence of this assumption was that little concern was shown for their customers – the various departments and organizations which were funded through the local authority – and no thought was given to becoming more efficient. They insisted on operating according to their own rigid procedures and would not entertain the idea of adjusting their way of working to suit a particular department's individual needs. This resulted in organizational innovations such as performance-related pay being blocked and the whole organization carrying the high overhead costs incurred by that department.

During the 1980s, three particular changes occurred: the introduction of competitive tendering to local government; the introduction of local management of schools; and the incorporation of further education colleges as independent of their local authority. The net effect of these changes meant that a significant proportion of the payroll department's customers began to have a choice. Some further education colleges and schools opted not to use the payroll department, on the grounds that they were too expensive and didn't meet their needs. Other departments began to demand similar choice and by the beginning of the 1990s, the council itself was even considering contracting out payroll services. What had seemed to be a comfortable, job-for-life department was now under threat.

The department fought against any change at first, but the economic reality was too apparent. Drastic action was needed and a new head of department set about initiating it. A first step was to encourage the payroll staff to participate in a number of council-wide customer care initiatives.

These required establishing a lead officer for customer care in each department. The lead officer received specific training, was provided with relevant training materials and was required to involve the whole department in quality circle-like teams, aimed to identify ways of improving customer care.

Another vital step introduced by the new head of department was that of asking the customers what they wanted and/or needed from a payroll department. The department defined what it was that they were offering and asked each customer which features were useful, and which new ones might be included. This went side-by-side with a major internal reappraisal, involving all of the staff. They looked at how the job could be done more cheaply and more efficiently, and at which of their own procedures were useful and which were not. The consequence was that a number of practices were shown to be outdated and unnecessary, and these were dropped.

The drastic reappraisal and change in the way of working and the involvement of the whole team (plus a certain amount of change in personnel through early retirement) brought about a dramatic change in attitude. From being a rigid, uncompromising and unfriendly department, payroll became entirely different. It was friendly to personal enquiries about pay, measured its effectiveness by customer surveys and embraced new technology to remove unecessary paper chasing. It also demonstrated how changing working practices for the benefit of their customers had actually reduced its costs.

The combination of wide-scale top-down organizational initiatives, bottom-up departmental problem-solving and a leadership emphasis on building an effective team through changing its values and orientation produced a department with a strong sense of pride in its work, and in its value to the local authority. Staff became proud of their dynamic approach to customer care and modern efficiency: a huge change from the situation in the same department just a few years earlier!

tantly – to listen thoughtfully to suggestions which come from other people.

Much organizational change is really about changing the culture of the organization as a whole. But as Davis (1985) showed, changing an organization's culture is something which also has to be done at the lower levels of a hierarchy. It simply isn't enough to develop new approaches at higher levels of management and expect them to filter downwards. No amount of rousing management talk is going to make any difference to a department which has dug in its heels and is doggedly resisting any changes. But involving some of those same people in cross-departmental project teams might just make a difference – if only by reducing their fear of the unknown. An organization based on team-working simply doesn't have the same type of inertia as an organization based on hierarchical authority because everyone, from the bottom upwards, has a much more direct involvement in the organization's goals and more interest in seeing that they are achieved.

According to Katzenbach and Smith, major organizational change requires three types of initiative which have to be implemented together, not one after the other. Top-down culture-shaping initiatives, emanating from senior management needs to occur at the same time as bottom-up goal achievement and problem-solving initatives, and also at the same time as cross-functional redesign and integration initiatives across the organization as a whole (See Table 6.4). Teams can be invaluable in establishing both the bottom-up initatives and the cross-cultural ones.

WHAT TEAMS NEED

So what do teams need from their organizations, if they are to function as a positive force within those organizations? Hackman (1990) identified six different types of organizational support which organizations can provide for their teams and which will help to make sure that the teams in the organization act as effectively and as efficiently as possible. These six areas apply pretty well to all teams, whether they are new-product teams, service teams, or organizational change teams. They help to make sure

Table 6.4 Types of initiative in major organizational change (adapted from Katzenbach and Smith 1993)

Top-down culture-shaping initatives	An organization needs to have a clear direction and aims when it is initiating organizational change. By bringing high-level executives together into a team with responsibility for identifying that direction and articulating the aims, the organization is able to initiate and negotiate effective organizational change. The team structure allows the organization to obtain widespread involvement from the top down.
Bottom-up goal achievement and problem-solving	While top-level support for organizational change is important, workshop and office-level teams have shown time and time again that they are vital in producing effective change that permeates the whole organization. By involving all of the work-force and drawing on their ideas and initiatives, organizations can generate a dynamic, and fully integrated, organizational culture.
Cross-functional redesign and integration initiatives.	Organizational change cannot be fully effective if it doesn't run across the whole organization. Team-based approaches can address this issue by drawing team members from different sectors of the organization. These teams can then ensure that the changes which are being proposed and implemented are structured in such a way as to have meaning across the whole organization, not just for particular sectors of the work-force.

that the organization and the team are closely in touch and that they stay that way throughout the team's life.

Clear targets

The first of these areas is to do with the team's targets. A team can't function properly without having a clearly defined task; and it is for the organization which created the team to make it clear what that task is. Failure to do so can produce serious problems. For example Shea (1986), in an analysis of the success or failure of quality circle projects, discovered that the unsuccessful ones were uncertain or confused about their purpose and looked in vain for guidance from their organization's culture.

A team's task itself can vary, from a single project to be

completed within a set period of time, like a new project development team, to a continuous purpose, such as a production team or a primary health care team. But no team can operate effectively unless its members know what its objectives are. Since it is the organization which establishes the team and provides resources for it, it is also the organization which needs to be clear about the purpose which the team is supposed to serve.

Adequate resources

A team cannot function effectively if it does not have the fundamental resources which it needs. These resources have to be provided by the organization in which the team is working. Resources can take many forms: a team needs financial resources, of course, but it may also need staffing resources, such as secretarial support. It needs a good mix of skills among the people who comprise the team, but it may also need suitable accommodation for meetings and so on. Each team has its own set of resource requirements and these are likely to change throughout the team's life. The organization needs to ensure that the necessary resources are available to the team, if it is to be able to carry out its task effectively.

Reliable information

If a team is to function well, it needs reliable information. It may need access to specific source material, or to find out how a particular process is undertaken or how a particular costing is obtained. Having accurate information can be vital if the team's decision-making is to be realistic, and it can also be essential in identifying when and where a problem may exist. A team has to be able to take into account new developments and changes in the organization around it and that needs information too. As we've just seen, successful teams don't just restrict their activities to internal processes: they also interact very closely with other parts of the organization, so changes in the organization can have a serious effect on how well the team itself is able to function. It is up to the organization, therefore, to make sure that a team has access to thorough, reliable information in order that it can work effectively.

Training and education

There is little point in assembling a team and then expecting that team to be able to carry out its task without any further training or education. Any organizational team, if it's working seriously, is likely to find that there are dimensions to its task which require additional skills or knowledge. It needs scope to take up training opportunities so that additional skills can be developed as and when they are required, rather than having the team muddle along with inadequate understanding. Having appropriate training and education available also makes it much easier for the team members to contribute fully to the team's task as they develop their expertise and awareness on an individual basis.

Education of this kind, though, isn't inevitably about courses. It's more a matter of continuous development and responding to new challenges, so it can take a lot of different forms. What is needed might be on-the-job-training, coaching from a supervisor, reading around a topic or distance learning, rather than short courses. It's up to the organization, though, to make sure that the team is able to obtain any training or education which it needs to carry out its task properly.

Regular feedback

Teams need regular and reliable feedback from their organization as they carry out their tasks. We've already seen how new project teams can fall apart if they don't maintain contact with other parts of the organization and that isn't simply a matter of diplomacy. It is also because they need to be able to learn from the rest of the organization; to adjust how the team works so that it can integrate more fully with other aspects of the organization; to know when it is doing something appropriately, so that it can retain that part of its task even if it is changing others; and, most importantly, to become aware of its achievements and what is yet to be done.

Organizational feedback, like training, can take a lot of forms. It may involve a regular bulletin on production figures, or on profits, made by the relevant part of the company. It may be information from quality of patient care surveys, expressions of approval from senior management, measures of customer satisfaction obtained by the sales teams or any of a host of different possibilities, depending on what the team is actually doing. But what is important is that the organization establishes systematic routes and procedures for the team to obtain regular feedback.

Technical and process assistance

Any working team will require a certain amount of technical support in order for it to carry out its task effectively. That might range from something as simple as having people who will produce slides or print copies of formal reports for a presentation, to needing someone who is able to provide detailed technical knowledge about the chemical stages involved in a particular production process. It might involve marketing specialists, who can advise the team on some of the marketing issues involved with bringing a new product onto the market; or it might involve bringing in an epidemiologist to advise the health care team on traffic accident patterns in a particular locality.

Unless it is constituted of unusually aware individuals, a team is also likely to need some process assistance – in other words, some help and know-how in getting things done in the organization itself. Organizations are complex beings and people working in one sector are often entirely unaware of how things are done in another part. So someone who is aware of what resources the organization has to offer, and how to go about obtaining particular bits of information, will make it very much easier for the team to do its job as efficiently as it possibly can.

The organization, then, is important to a working team; and if we are to understand the full implications of this we also need to understand something about how organizations themselves work. That doesn't mean exploring detailed structures and chains of command – that would be fairly pointless, since each organization has its own distinctive pattern. Rather, it involves understanding something of the more subtle social factors which influence organizational cultures and how people participate in them, so that we can understand some of the psychological processes influencing the way that teams and their organizations interact. We will do this in the next chapter.

SUMMARY

- Research has shown that the way that teams interact with their organizations can be vital for their effectiveness or success. This interaction can take many different forms and does not just involve the team's leader.
- Organizational support for teamwork is essential. Organizations which are supportive of teamwork often have a relatively 'flat' shape and a culture which includes trust and confidence in employees.
- Theories of organizational culture range from typologies, semiotic and systems analysis to models of culture as shared beliefs. The current model is layered, with a manifest level of symbols and other signs, a strategic level of distinctive practices and a core level of deeply-held beliefs and assumptions.
- It is useful to see organizational cultures as networks of working groups, teams and departments, any of which may share the organization's culture to a greater or lesser degree. This approach highlights the importance of social identification and the role of teams.
- Competition between teams has to be carefully managed so as to ensure that it is competition about achievement rather than competition about organizational resources. The one can promote positive, friendly rivalry; the other promotes political manoevering and intergroup hostility.
- Teams can be a major force in organizational change: partly because their own approaches and values can represent positive directions for change and partly through the way that they interact with the organization as a whole.
- Teams require six things from their organizations if they are to function effectively: clear targets, adequate resources, reliable information, training and education, regular feedback and technical or process assistance.

Box 6.4   **Management recommendations**

Ensure that the team includes people who understand the need for ambassadorial as well as task-co-ordinator activities on the part of the team.

Chart the six types of organizational support which teams need and go through them with the team leader, to ensure that the team has the resources and support it needs to function properly.

Examine carefully how far the expressed cultural values of the organization, as expressed in mission statements, co-ordinate with the expressed goals and values of the team. Discuss any mismatches at higher levels as well as with the team itself.

Make sure that competition between teams or departments is based on achievement only, and think about establishing competitions of this kind if they do not exist. Eliminate all competition for resources as far as possible.

Make sure that change initiatives in the organization are discussed and modified from the bottom up, and across departments or functions, so that they do not just arrive downwards from the higher levels of the organization.

7 Teams, organizations and innovation

The last chapter discussed how teams can be a vital force for implementing organizational change. But teams don't just help organizations to implement changes of policy. In an organization which has adopted a teamworking philosophy, a great deal of organizational change can come from the accumulated actions of the teams themselves.

INNOVATIVE TEAMS AT WORK

As we saw in Chapter 1, the Japanese philosophy of *kaizen* is all about continuous organizational change, not through single big jumps, but through constantly making little improvements and adjustments to how things are done. In the Japanese model, these improvements come directly from the working teams themselves: they are always considering new ideas, evaluating them and testing them out. Indeed, thinking of and suggesting improvements is considered to be as much a part of work routine as actually performing the tasks themselves. And the combined outcome of these continual small adjustments is that the organization itself is constantly changing.

Features of innovative teams

But this does not mean that Japanese people, as individuals, are necessarily more innovative than Westerners. Individual differences in personality don't seem to exert a great deal of influence on whether a team approaches its work in an innovative manner or not. West and Wallace (1991) studied a set of eight primary health care teams – teams consisting of doctors, nurses and health visitors who were responsible for general medical care in the population. Five of those teams were judged to be 'innovative' in the way that they worked, while three were 'traditional', according to the assessments of a research health visitor and a hospital registrar who were familiar with each team.

The researchers investigated several different variables, which included information about the team's characteristics and also measures of individual factors, such as how personally innovative each team member was. What they found, interestingly enough, was that the individual factors had no relationship at all to how innovative the team itself was. Someone could be very innovative in the way that they carried out their own personal role, but this didn't mean that the team they belonged to would also act in an innovative manner.

What made the difference to the teams, West and Wallace found, were three sets of variables. One of these was what they referred to as the **climate** of the team: whether the team tolerated different approaches, encouraged new ideas and supported a controlled level of experimentation. We explored this variable to some degree when we looked at the Team Climate Inventory in Chapter 5, and we will be coming back to it later in this chapter.

A second variable was to do with the degree of **commitment** shown by members of the team: whether people felt they wanted to remain in the team, whether they shared the values and goals of the team and whether they were willing to put effort into the team projects. As we've seen, commitment is linked very closely with the question of social identification and whether people feel strongly that they 'belong' to the team, and share its values. And the third factor was to do with **collaboration**: whether the team had open communication and people shared information willingly, whether there was mutual trust between the members and whether they tended to sort out conflicts by discussing them openly and reaching a consensus.

Of course, it isn't possible to tell which comes first: whether the team becomes innovative because it has these characteristics, or whether the process of being innovative leads the team to develop them. Most likely, as with so many human issues, there's a two-way relationship between the two. But West and Wallace's research tells us two things: first, that individual characteristics are probably not as important as we might assume; and second, that climate, commitment and collaboration are the qualities which we need to foster in a team if we want to encourage it to be dynamic and innovative.

Team factors contributing to organizational change

Teams can be a vital factor in larger organizational changes too – indeed, as we've seen, some researchers believe that teams are absolutely necessary for successful organizational innovation. Anderson, Hardy and West (1990) explored the characteristics of innovative teams at work and identified four important factors which allow a team to be a positive, dynamic force for change within an organization: vision, participative safety, climate for excellence and support for innovation. Table 7.1 lists these factors, along with an explanation of each one.

The importance of **vision** has come up on more than one occasion throughout this book and is likely to come up again, too. In Chapter 3, we saw how the establishment of a shared vision which can generate clear and mutually understood aims is fundamental in effective team-building. In Chapter 4, we looked at how important it was for leaders, too, to maintain a clear vision if they were to maintain direction and morale among their teams. And vision is equally important in organizational innovation: a clear, openly discussed vision provides a positive target for innovation and makes it easier to adopt and to evaluate initiatives.

But above all, it is vital that this vision is shared by all of those involved in establishing organizational change, or carrying through innovations. As Anderson, Hardy and West (1990) observed – and we can see why from Chapter 6 – a vision which has been imposed from the top is unlikely to be successful. People are only likely to act in accordance with a particular vision if they agree with it and feel that to some extent they 'own' it.

Like several other researchers in this field, Anderson, Hardy and West (1990) argue that truly effective organizational innovation only really occurs at the level of the working group or team. It cannot be established arbitrarily by management, if it is to work fully. People need to feel that they have been actively involved in

Table 7.1   Factors in innovative teams (adapted from Anderson, Hardy and West 1990)

Vision	This concerns the question of whether the team has a clearly articulated idea about its ultimate purpose or goals. This may take the form of a mission statement, a formal set of objectives, or simply a clearly shared and openly discussed vision of the future.
Participative safety	This is about whether the atmosphere within the group or team is such that people feel able to contribute ideas or to challenge existing practices without feeling threatened. Going against established wisdom or commonly-accepted viewpoints can be a difficult thing to do, and it is only likely to happen as a matter of course in a working climate of trust, warmth, participation and free sharing of information.
Climate for excellence	This is about whether the working atmosphere is such that people are clearly focused on doing their job in the best way possible. It requires an openness to ideas for improvement, constant vigilance about maintaining high standards, and a willingness to think constructively about criticisms without becoming defensive.
Support for innovation	This is to do with how the team or group tackles new ideas and alternative approaches to what they are doing. It concerns whether new ideas are taken seriously, tried out, and provided with appropriate time and resources, rather than simply being dismissed by the group or its leader without being tested.

forming and negotiating innovations, and they need to be satisfied that they really will produce improvement.

Since working groups change, as people leave or move on and new people join the department, this means that the shared vision itself will need to be continually re-negotiated. As a result, it is likely to evolve, continually and in subtle ways, in order to reflect the perceptions and values of those who are trying to realize it. And this underlines the importance of the vision being clearly and explicitly stated, rather than taken for granted by management or team leaders.

As we saw in the last chapter, working groups can either be a source of resistance to change, or a source of innovation in themselves. Anderson, Hardy and West identified **participative safety** as an important element in reducing the amount of resistance to change. If people really do feel able to participate in decision-making processes, to share information and to offer ideas for better ways of working, then they are most unlikely to resist change just for the sake of it.

But establishing participative safety isn't as easy as it might seem. Meetings, votes, exchanges of information and other participation mechanisms can be exactly what they appear: a chance for the individual to participate. Or they can be subtle forms of political or personal manoeuvring, in which employees know very well that speaking their mind can produce extremely unfavourable consequences. It is possible to have all the forms of participation, with none of the safety. But if innovation is to be possible, people need to feel able to propose ideas which are different and challenging, without leaving themselves open to ridicule, censorship, or vindictiveness from others.

Having a **climate for excellence** is another factor which reduces resistance to change. It means making a real commitment to establishing first-class practices, procedures and standards of work. It's easy to detect: do the team discuss the quality of their work and monitor how well they are getting on? Do they explore ways of improving their standards or achieving their objectives? Do they engage in critical appraisal of their own performance and seek ways that they can improve it? Are individuals encouraged by the rest of the team to try out new ideas if they want to? All of these are clear messages that a climate for excellence either exists, or is developing, within a team. And such a climate provides the spur that is needed for innovation – it makes it easy for teams to change and adapt, because new practices are seen as helping them to do the job as well as possible.

But as with participative safety, the real thing can sometimes become obscured. Some groups or departments may look as though they aim to maintain a climate for excellence, but really do the opposite. A group may develop a vocabulary and style of conversation which implies that they are at the forefront of their work, while really masking a static, complacent approach which is highly resistant to any real change. Alternatively, an organization may profess to aim for excellence, but refuse to allow its teams to invest in training or facilities which would enable them to improve what they are doing.

Sometimes, too, institutional practices designed to establish a climate for excellence may have the opposite effect. Monitoring performance is an important basis for improving it, but the adoption of an inappropriate appraisal system can too easily mean that only pedestrian, unimaginative forms of working are actually recognized and rewarded, while innovative approaches and new ideas are not given credit. In their team innovation checklist (Table 7.2) Anderson, Hardy and West suggest that one way of detecting the real from the false is to find out whether the team members are really prepared to discuss opposing ideas fully. It's a useful indicator of whether the climate for excellence is real, or just a superficial facade.

And then there's the question of whether there really is **support for innovation**, in the team and in the organization as a whole. If a team is to be innovative, it is important that its members see innovation as something which is desirable. That may seem obvious, but it isn't something which can be taken for granted. It is important that team members encourage and support new ideas. Offering practical help, listening and taking ideas seriously and co-operating with new procedures are all manifestations of whether the team itself is supporting innovation.

In the organizational context, the question becomes even more significant. Most organizations insist that they encourage their staff to be innovative and that they welcome new ideas from employees. But far fewer create a working context where innovations are actually supported. Indeed, in many organizations it is likely that an innovative approach will be actively blocked by management – either deliberately, as managers react to what they see as a 'threat' to their control, or unconsciously through restrictive administrative or bureaucratic practices. Senior executives in an organization can do a great deal to facilitate innovation emerging from working teams, but they can impede them even more easily by professing to support the innovation but failing to provide practical help or to make their support clear in other parts of the organization.

Table 7.2   Team innovation checklist (source: Anderson, Hardy and West 1990)

Vision	Does the team have a clearly articulated vision, mission or set of objectives? Is the vision or set of objectives clearly stated? Was the vision (or set of objectives) originally developed and negotiated by the whole team? Is this vision (or set of objectives) attainable?
Participative safety	Do team members share information fully with each other? Do all team members participate in decision-making? Are team members ready to propose new ideas which challenge existing ways of doing things? Do team members discuss each other's work-related anxieties and successes? Is there a climate of trust and warmth within the group?
Climate for excellence	Is excellent team performance of central importance to the team? What procedures and methods are used to monitor and improve performance levels? Are all team members committed to excellent standards? Are team members prepared to discuss opposing ideas fully?
Support for innovation	Do team members support new ideas? Do team members give time, co-operation and resources to help each other implement new ideas? Does the team leader support and encourage new ideas? Does the team leader offer practical help and resources for the development of new ideas?

These four factors: vision, participative safety, climate for excellence and support for innovation may seem to bear a striking resemblance to the four factors underpinning the Team Climate Inventory which we looked at in Chapter 5. That is not a coincidence. The research reported by Anderson, Hardy and West was one of the many projects which formed the theoretical foundations of the Team Climate Inventory, and which helped to identify and firm up the four fundamental factors which it assesses. The checklist in Table 7.2 is not intended to replace the Inventory – indeed,

Box 7.1 **Support for innovation**

Although management theorists have been advising managers that it makes sense to empower staff for several decades, a surprising number of high-level managers in Britain still seem to belong to the 'old school', adopting an autocratic and often deliberately divisive approach to their subordinate departments. Their belief appears to be that while staff are in conflict with one another, they are unlikely to focus discontent on their top management. But this is a very short-term policy and one which does not benefit the organization in the long run.

This was very clearly illustrated by the management policies of two further education colleges. Although the work of the two colleges was very similar, each being based in a middle-sized industrial town and running courses which served the needs of their community, the approaches adopted by the two college principals were entirely different. In the first, which we shall call Oldtown College, the principal was of the 'old school'. He adopted a deliberate policy of 'divide and rule' with the various departments of the college, setting them in competition with one another for resources and subtly encouraging behind-the-scenes political maneouvring. By controlling budgets and allocations, he was able to determine matters such as the number of new staff which the college could employ, and heads of departments were encouraged to compete for them – although the precise criteria for the competition were never specified. The heads of departments divined, quite accurately, that it was really a matter of being in the principal's favour.

In the second, which we shall call Townbridge College, the principal adopted an upfront, largely market-based approach to resourcing. Staffing and resource decisions were made largely on the basis of course enrolments: the more students a department had, the more staff it earned – a logical policy to any outsider and one which was focused towards enabling the college to grow in an effective manner. At the same time, money and opportunities were made available for staff to open up new ways of working: whether these were accepted depended mainly on the strength of the case which was made when applying for the money and the potential for growth if the new idea worked out. As a result, the staff worked hard to build up their courses and to develop new ones; and promotional criteria were based firmly on individual achievement.

As one might expect, the two colleges, ostensibly so similar in terms of their work and markets, were very different indeed. The working atmosphere in Oldtown College was fine on a day to day basis, but there were many tensions under the surface and these would become more visible at times of stress, in the form of back-biting and political game-playing. This situation, understandably, generated a certain amount of insecurity on the part of many staff, and produced a reluctance to engage in anything other than conventional teaching – even though the external educational environment was changing dramatically. There was a high level of staff turnover, and not a random one at that, in that the college tended to lose many of its most dynamic and innovative staff after relatively few years. They were aware that their only chance of promotion was to become political game-players and many of them were simply not prepared to do so.

Townbridge College, on the other hand, dealt with the changing educational environment very positively. By rewarding its innovators and competent teachers, it had retained its best staff and opened up areas of vocational education which had not previously existed. The working atmosphere was relatively straightforward: although there were the inevitable conflicts between individuals, there was little of the systematic maneouvring and game-playing which was so apparent in Oldtown College. Staff were able to take pride in their work and became actively involved in many of the educational changes which were going on. Moreover, they were able to develop their courses knowing that if a new course did catch on and become popular, that it would be resourced effectively. In other words, the atmosphere at the college was dynamic, optimistic and innovative, and the contrast between it and Oldtown College was quite remarkable.

it would not be able to. But it can provide a brief managerial guide to the kinds of questions which need to be addressed in establishing support for innovation.

HOW A TEAM CAN INFLUENCE AN ORGANIZATION

I have talked a lot about how teams can influence their organizations. But organizations, for the most part, tend to be large and diverse. Teams, on the other hand, tend to be small and well-defined. So, almost by definition, any one team will only consist of a very small proportion of the organization's employees. On the surface, therefore, it would seem to be impractical for such a small minority to attempt to influence the organization as a whole. Being outnumbered, being counted as 'different', and the sheer inertia of large numbers of people would seem to mean that any attempt by the team to change how the organization works would be doomed to failure from the outset.

Minority influence

But it doesn't actually work like that. Actually, minorities can have a great deal of influence, even when they are hopelessly outnumbered. After all, each of the great social reforms, such as the abolition of slavery or the factory reform acts in the nineteenth century began with the determined campaigning of a very small number of people against a massive complacency on the part of most of the powerful sectors of that society. With a combination of vision, consistency and articulate argument, almost anything becomes possible.

In a series of studies, Moscovici and other researchers (e.g. Moscovici and Lage 1976) showed that even in situations where majority influence appears to be very powerful, it is possible for minorities to have a considerable effect. An important factor in producing that effect, it emerged, was consistency. Moscovici found that as long as the minority group were consistent in the way that they argued and didn't differ openly among themselves, they could eventually change the majority view, so that others came around to their way of thinking despite the pressures to conform to the majority.

Nemeth and Wachtler (1974), also looked at this area and found that even one person could change the ideas or decisions of a majority group. Their research showed that it was important that the person should be reasonably consistent, but that it was even more important that they should appear to be autonomous – to be able to make their own choices. In a simulated jury-decision experiment, for instance, a single person who had chosen to sit in a conspicuous place was able to change the entire group's verdict, but that person's influence was totally diminished if they had been told where to sit.

Although this might seem trivial, it tells us something quite significant about minority influence. It tells us that the most important thing about minority influence is that the people in the majority should be able to respect those putting the minority view. Indeed, other researchers have shown that the minority's influence appears to occur mainly because the minority is seen as producing a more 'truthful' argument: one which they have chosen to adopt and in which they believe (Perez and Mugny 1987). Seemingly unimportant things like choosing one's own seat are taken as indicators of the person's independence and as implying that the person is acting voluntarily, according to their own principles. Acquiescing when told where to sit, on the other hand, signifies a less autonomous individual and, by association, a less independent or autonomous point of view.

That doesn't mean, of course, that all minorities are equally influential. Social identification comes in here as well, because if someone is seen as being an 'outsider', with entirely different interests, then they can be as consistent and independent as they want, but they are not likely to have much of an effect. Hogg and Abrams (1993) discussed how influential minorities actually take great pains to reassure majority group members that they are not really acting in opposition to the group, but instead share the majority's overall beliefs and ideals. By doing this, they prevent the discussion from becoming polarized into a 'them-and-us' debate. As a result, these influential minorities make sure that the majority group members are able to consider their ideas without feeling that they are acting against their own group's interest if they do.

Characteristics of innovative teams

An awareness of how minority influence works also helps us to understand something about what a team needs, if it is to become a dynamic force within its organization. West (1995) identified five characteristics which a team needs if it is to become an instrument for change. The first of these, as you may have guessed by now, is that the team needs to have a **clear vision** of what it is trying to achieve. The goal must be something that all of the team members want, and that they are prepared to put effort into achieving. That might sound obvious on paper, but too often, teams tend to take it for granted that everyone has the same goals without actually making sure that their vision is fully shared.

The second team need is adequate and consistent **communication**. The vision needs to be put across to other people clearly and articulately. As we've already seen, disagreements among the minority group's members will reduce their potential for influencing the majority. So it is important that all team members are seen to be putting the same message across. And it is equally important that the people they are talking to can perceive, fully, what the message is all about. Again, that might sound obvious, but it is often surprisingly difficult to explain something which you have spent a great deal of time working out. There are often assumptions underlying a change proposal which those who have been working on it have come to take for granted. But they need to be spelt out to other people who have not been through the development process.

The third requirement for minority influence in organizations is **flexibility**. As we've seen, a minority isn't likely to make much difference if it becomes classified as a set of 'outsiders', and sticking to a fixed, rigid approach makes that very likely. It is important that the team is flexible enough to be able to respond to the concerns and suggestions of other people working in the organization. Indeed, doing so is an important part of reassuring the majority that the team is actually working in the organization's best interests. And the team needs to recognize that it doesn't have a monopoly on ideas: it is very likely that non-team members, too, will be able to contribute important experience or useful suggestions which can help in the implementation of the change.

The fourth characteristic which West identified as important for a successfully innovative team is that of **persistence**. The psychological research into minority influence shows us how sticking to the same line is absolutely vital. Changing one's mind without explaining why, or arbitrarily proposing a new direction, is likely to lose any influence that has already been gained – and in a way which makes it very difficult to regain the ground which has been lost. On the surface, this might seem as though it contradicts the previous characteristic about the need to be flexible, but it doesn't really. It's one thing being prepared to adapt and take additional information into account, but it's a different thing to change direction or give up altogether. A team which wants to make a difference to its organization must be prepared to be persistent – to give the same message over and over again, even when it seems futile. Only consistent and repeated persuasion is likely to produce an effect.

West's fifth characteristic of successfully innovative teams is that of **participation**. It isn't enough simply that all of the team members are involved in proposed change. If a team really wants to change how an organization works, it also needs to involve other people in that change. Everyone who becomes involved enough to contribute an idea, or to test out a new way of working, is one less person who opposes the team's ideas. The more people who share in the change process, the more widely accepted those ideas will become in the organization and the less resistance the team will have to overcome.

All this is not to say that it will be easy for a team to produce change in its organization. Inevitably, change produces conflict and a lot of people find that very threatening. But real boats do rock and an organization which opposes all change routinely is an organization which has become stagnant and complacent. Survival in the modern world involves being able to adapt to new demands and new ways of working. On the surface, to other members of the organization, a challenging team might seem like a group of trouble-makers, just out to disrupt everyone's comfortable life. But underneath, they are likely to be the organization's main source of creativity and innovation. It is important, though, that the team members understand that they are likely to meet with resistance and conflict as they go ahead with their plans.

RESISTANCE TO TEAMWORKING

As we've seen, then, teams can be a powerful force for change in their organizations. They can be a source of organizational dynamism and profit and, they can be a significant source of organizational and professional pride. But they can also fail to work. A great many organizations claim to have introduced teamworking and yet an examination of their working practices shows little of these outcomes.

With all of the evidence about the positive benefits that teamworking can produce, it might be expected that every organization would be shifting over to teamworking as fast as it can. But there are also factors within the organization itself which can produce resistance to teams and teamworking. Katzenbach and Smith (1993) discussed three reasons why an organization may be resistant to teams.

Lack of belief in teamworking

The first of these is simply a lack of conviction that teamworking will actually make any difference. That lack of conviction can come from many sources. Some people simply believe that individuals work better, and are less troublesome to manage, than teams. To some managers, the time which teams spend in defining goals, discussing approaches, and looking at alternatives appears to be a waste of time, which would not be necessary if people were getting on with their individual jobs. Other managers see teams as largely a human-relations exercise, but not one which has much to do with productivity. They are sceptical about the value of looking for agreement or consensus, because they do not feel that this inevitably leads to the best possible solutions.

And there are grounds for all of these fears. As we have seen, effective teams need clear direction, articulated values and visions, a positive task orientation, resources and numerous other factors. Without these, a group of people who are labelled a team can actually be less effective than those individuals might be if they were working on their own – in the same way that a committee can take much longer to come to the same conclusions as a working party of two or three individuals. So a team which spends time on these issues without actually achieving consensus on vision, task orientation and so on may indeed be using organizational time unproductively.

But that is what successful team management is all about. It is about making sure that a particular set of people actually does operate as a team – that its members act positively and dynamically to achieve the team's goals, rather than acting as a group or discussion circle. The numerous factors in team management which we have explored throughout this book, and the management recommendations at the end of each chapter, are important pointers for achieving this.

Part of the problem, though, is that people are often very vague about what they mean when they talk of a 'team'. They use the word as if it were synonymous with a working group, or sometimes even as if the whole organization could be regarded as a team. As we saw in Chapter 2, a team is quite different from a group. Teams are not just about having shared values or ideas: they are, in Katzenbach and Smith's terms, discrete units of performance: small groups of people with complementary skills, who are committed to a common purpose and a set of specific performance goals. Anything less than that is simply not a team.

Personal threat and anxiety

The second source of organizational resistance to teams comes from the idea that teamworking, if people are not used to it, can be personally uncomfortable. Most of us, by and large, are used to looking after our own work in organizations and trying to keep control over what we do. Sharing that control with other people and becoming dependent on others to achieve working goals can be quite threatening. It takes some time to build up trust between team members and the benefits of that trust are not always apparent from the outset. For some people, teamworking just doesn't look as though it will make their organizational life any easier, or any more productive.

Teamworking can also be threatening on a personal level. People may feel vulnerable at the idea of their weaknesses and mistakes exposed to the scrutiny of other team members. They may not feel able to speak out in a group or share their own ideas, in case those ideas are ridiculed or regarded as inadequate. Such activities require a certain amount of self-confidence and self-confidence doesn't necessarily go hand in hand with doing a job well. Some people are perfectly competent at their own individual job, but find it very difficult to have to interact with other people at the level which is required for successful teamwork.

As Hackman (1994) pointed out, it is usually necessary for an organization to train people explicitly in teamworking skills. And it is important to remember that doing so might also mean that deeper anxieties and insecurities need to be tackled. Of course, the evidence is that the positive side of belonging to, and being accepted by, a positive team can go a long way towards remedying personal insecurity, but that doesn't help someone with this problem who is contemplating a change to teamworking. The initial resistance to teamwork has to be overcome first and the main way to do that is with explicit training in teamworking skills.

Organizational resistance

A third source of resistance to teams may lie in the organization itself. As we've seen, effective teamwork can mean that the organization performs much more efficiently. But some organizations simply don't operate with a particularly strong commitment to high performance. Although they almost always pay lip-service to the importance of performance, the directors of such organizations don't really think that it is worth changing their ways of working to make sure that the organization does perform more efficiently. They make vague statements but don't actually bring them into practice in terms of what their employees actually do. And Chapter 6 showed us that what the employees and working groups actually do is the core of organizational effectiveness.

Classic hierarchical organizations can sometimes become deeply ineffectual, without those at the top actually realizing it. When each decision has to pass upwards through the hierarchy, and only the top levels are seen as able to initiate anything important, efficient performance doesn't have top priority – after all, it is likely to involve responding to change and that means making decisions. Instead, people working in organizations like that tend to try to make sure that their own job remains consistent, with as little change or threat as possible.

Sadly, the story of Sheetrock Inc. in Box 7.2 is not the only example of an organization which has attempted to introduce teamworking without making it possible for the teams actually to work. Table 7.3 describes six factors which can inhibit teams from functioning positively within their organization. Teamwork inevitably involves giving autonomy and decision-making to people who may not even be particularly senior in terms of the organization's hierarchy. But Katzenbach and Smith argue that it is quite pointless trying to introduce teamworking to an organization, unless that organization has what they refer to as 'a

Box 7.2 **Organizational resistance to teamworking**

Glover (1992) reported on what happened at an organization referred to as 'Sheetrock Inc.'. This was a large American organization which originally had a reputation for building high-quality housing. In the 1970s, however, the organization was run by a different set of directors who believed very firmly in rigid Theory X-type management styles and who developed the company into one which produced a high turnover of low-quality housing.

This company consciously employed team-building as part of their organizational development. But this was not team-building based on respect for the employees. The teams met on a weekly basis, after work for two or three hours, with attendance being compulsory and monitored. Employee performance was discussed and any deficiencies were made public. The team meetings emphasized the rewards of obedience and the consequences of failure, and were designed to ensure that employees were kept in line through aggressive manipulation. They also emphasized a 'the company is important, not me' attitude, with employees even being instructed to refer to 'the desk the company allows me to use' rather than 'my desk'. One person even bought his own office furniture so that he could refer to it as 'my' desk.

The directors deliberately recruited top executives and managers who were high on machiavellianism (that is, who were manipulative, power-oriented and ruthless), in the belief that these were the people who would be most effective at generating a high performance ethic in the organization. They encouraged their performance by bonus schemes based on productivity, which acted against high-quality work and also gave the company problems when it hit financial difficulties, since its executives acted for personal reward and not for the sake of the company.

The directors also established an internal audit department, whose real role was to act as a kind of 'secret police', monitoring the telephone calls and other behaviour of employees and looking for abuses of company time or resources. Although organizational consultants tried to steer them towards a more positive course, they ignored any proposals except those which they could incorporate into their existing approach.

For the first few years, the company was extremely successful and expanded into a national organization. But this was at a time of general economic growth. When the market changed, the company's coercive and highly controlled policies meant that it was unable to respond. Eventually the organization crashed badly. The machiavellian management style had produced high employee turnover and no company loyalty; their over-controlled style meant that they had no mechanism for listening to their employees and so becoming aware of market changes before disaster struck; and their executive recruitment policy, which had emphasized machiavellian qualities meant that they did not have managers with knowledge of alternative approaches available.

(Source: Glover 1992)

robust performance ethic'. If it doesn't, then teams will not be welcome and organizational and personal resistance to them will ensure that they are not likely to be able to achieve much anyway.

WHEN TEAMS DON'T WORK

As we've seen, using a team-centred approach within a company can provide a dynamic force for innovation and change, which can help an organization to act and react positively within its environment. But establishing a team-centred approach in an organization doesn't just consist of allocating new jobs to groups of people and expecting them to act together. As we've seen, teams require resources, feedback and commitment from their organizations if they are to act effectively.

And teams also require trust. If the team is to make its own decisions about its work, then the manager of that section, by definition, has less control over what those decisions actually are. Hackman (1990) pointed out that adopting a team-based approach throughout an organization is actually a revolutionary

Table 7.3 Inhibiting factors in team performance (source: Katzenbach and Smith 1993)

Lack of autonomy	The team needs to be able to make its own decisions about how it carries out its work, and will not be able to function well if its decisions are frequently overruled or interfered with.
Lack of support and commitment	The team needs support from individuals higher up in the organization. It also needs organizational commitment to its project, so that it will be able to carry through its task effectively.
The team is too large	A team which is too large will not able to engage all its members fully, and will encourage 'social loafing', or some members not participating to their fullest extent.
Lack of resources	A team cannot function effectively if it is unable to obtain the resources or training that it needs.
Lack of feedback / recognition	People become demoralized faced with a continual feeling of failure or frustration. Teams need to have their positive achievements reflected back to them from time to time.
Competitive individual appraisal	Appraisal systems which put the team members in competition with one another, or which fail to recognize the achievements of the team as a whole, undermine the co-operative dimensions of teamwork and can be extremely demoralizing to team members.

change and one which many organizations are not actually prepared to undertake. Creating team-centred organizations inevitably involves a certain amount of risk, since the team will not operate effectively if it is not allowed control over its operation. There is always the possibility that what the team decides to do may not actually be in the best interest of the organization as a whole.

We have seen earlier in this book how that type of danger is minimized when the team has a clear vision and is set clear targets from the organization. As we saw in Chapter 4, effective team management provides a framework within which the teams operate, sets clear goals for the teams to achieve and provides the team with the resources and skill mix which it needs to carry out its task. But, as Hackman (1994) pointed out, too many organizations simply jump on the 'teamwork' bandwagon without really thinking these issues through. And in these organizations, inevitably, their team structure doesn't really work.

Tripwires in implementing teamwork

Hackman described five common pitfalls, which he referred to as 'tripwires', which are found in organizations which believe that they are implementing a positive team-centred approach, while they are really (but unconsciously) sabotaging it. The tripwires are listed in Table 7.4, but we will discuss them in a little more detail here as well, since, by showing us what organizations can do wrong, they also give us useful hints about what organizations can do right.

The first trip-wire which Hackman identified is when managers call a performing unit a team, but really manage it as a set of individuals. This is all to do with how the achievements of the team are appraised, how the team members' own performance is judged and whether the team members are seen as interdependent in carrying out their work, or whether management just sees each one as working separately with their own little piece of the jigsaw.

Reward is not the only issue here. Hackman pointed out that a real team (as opposed to a group of individuals who are being called a team) has three distinctive characteristics. The first of

Table 7.4   Hackman's five trip-wires (source: Hackman 1994)

1. That managers call a performing unit a team, but really manage it as a set of individuals.
2. Imposing too much or too little authority.
3. The tendency to tear down organizational structures.
4. Skimping on organizational supports.
5. Assuming staff are eager to work in teams and that they are already skilled at doing so.

these is that it is clear where the team begins and ends – who belongs to it and who doesn't – and although that may change over time, for the most part the team is relatively stable. The second is that team members share common goals, but also depend on each other in working towards them; and the third is that the team has the autonomy to manage its own work and internal processes. Without these three characteristics, it isn't really practical to consider a working group as a team, in any dynamic sense.

Hackman described his second tripwire as 'falling off the authority balance beam'. What he meant by using this metaphor is that an organization using teamwork has to perform a balancing act between over-controlling the teams or giving them too much autonomy. Both of these can be damaging. Being over-controlled, as we have seen, means that the team will not be able to make the day to day decisions which it needs to work effectively. But having no direction or control at all can mean that the team turns off and becomes apathetic, or that it becomes anarchic, taking off in its own direction without considering the organization as a whole.

There's a balance which needs to be drawn between the two extremes and Hackman identifies this as being to do with whether the team's management specifies means (how the team should do its work) or ends (the results which they should achieve). The outcome of these is shown in Figure 7.1. A real, effective team in Hackman's view needs to have definite direction and this is brought about by making it clear what the ends should be, but leaving the team to decide for itself the means which it will use to attain those ends.

Another 'tripwire' which Hackman identified is the tendency of some organizations to tear down as many of the existing organizational structures as they possibly can, when deciding to adopt a team-centred approach. Typically, Hackman argues, the management of an organization doing this will assemble a large group of people, tell them what needs to be accomplished and let them 'work out the details' for themselves. The problem, though, is that team members can't work everything out on their own: they need a set of structures within which to work. If it is trying to establish positive teamworking, an organization needs to maintain enabling structures which will help teams to work effectively.

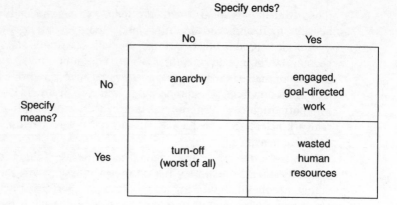

Figure 7.1   The authority balance beam (Source: Hackman 1994)

It isn't the organizational structures by themselves which will interfere with team operation. The key points for effective teams in this respect, Hackman argues, are a well-designed team task which will motivate the team members; a well-composed team; and a clear specification of the core norms of conduct which are expected from team members – what team members should 'always' do and what they should 'never' do. Those are necessary for the team, but as long as what they are doing, and their right to do it, is acknowledged, a team can function positively within existing organizational structures. Indeed, it is more likely to do so than if they have to establish everything from scratch.

A different tripwire which can interfere with teamwork in an organization is if it is skimping on organizational supports. As we've seen earlier, an effective team needs to operate within a supportive organizational context. Hackman describes such a context as having an appropriate reward system within the organization, an appropriate educational system (which will provide training and self-learning opportunities where needed), an appropriate information system, so that team members are aware of what is happening within the organization and can communicate with others, and sufficient material resources with which to operate effectively. It is pointless, he argues, to expect teams to work positively if they don't have these fundamental features of support from their organization.

The fifth tripwire which Hackman identified is that of assuming that the organization's staff are eager to work in teams and that they are already skilled at doing so. People are often unfamiliar with teamwork and may be resistant to it at first – after all, it is quite different from the individualistic approaches to work with which most people in Western cultures are brought up. At the very least, staff often need specific training to help them to engage in teamwork effectively. Ignoring this, or taking it for granted, can mean that teams fall apart or become damaged by interpersonal conflicts and rivalries.

Instead, Hackman argues, the team's leader or manager must actively coach the team in the skills needed to work well in a team. Each leader will choose their own way of doing this, but Hackman sees it as being as much a part of a team leader's job as creating opportunities for favourable performance by the team and building up the team as a performance unit. The team leader needs to choose the right times – times when the team isn't working flat out and so has a bit of opportunity to reflect – and consciously focus on activities which will help to train the team members in working together and sharing responsibility. That might involve anything from discussing the team's experiences to engaging in structured exercises, depending on how the team leader prefers to work. By doing this, the team will have a good chance of becoming welded into an effective working group.

Establishing team effectiveness

What this all adds up to, as Hackman (1990) made clear, is that the overall conditions for team effectiveness within an organization involve having a real team, with a clear direction and an enabling team structure, operating within a supportive organizational context and with expert coaching in teamwork available. Each of the elements here is something which needs to be thought through by an organization introducing teamwork. A team can have all of the characteristics and coaching it needs, but it won't realize its potential if it is trying to operate in an unsupportive organizational context. Similarly, it is pointless expecting a team to be able to operate fully if it doesn't really know what it is trying to achieve, or if it doesn't have any opportunity to learn the teamworking skills which will be necessary.

According to Hackman, however, many organizations which

Box 7.3   **Team Values**

As we've seen so often in this book, one of the most important things in any organization is that people should have a
clear sense of what they are doing, and why it matters. It is
that clarity which allows people to act efficiently: without it,
an organization needs to keep constant supervision over
what its staff are doing and cannot allow its members to
use their own judgement, in case they act in ways that are
entirely inappropriate. But with it, each person is able to
contribute their own part to the whole enterprise, knowing
that what they are doing is appropriate and that it is in
accordance with the organization's values and objectives.

When a small business is first established, its founders are
usually very clear about their aims and values. As the company grows, however, it takes on new staff and they, inevitably, are less well-informed. One such organization,
Concorde Informatics, had grown to employ about 25 people
when it began a consultancy project aimed at introducing the
company's management to the need for communication of
clear team values through the company.

It was apparent from the outset that the directors of the
company had a thoughtful and visionary approach to its
development – indeed, that was why they had engaged in
the consultancy project in the first place. They planned for
the company to grow, but to do so in a well-founded and
secure manner. They also had very clear values, including
extremely high professional working standards, a planned
strategy for the development of the business and a positive
belief in their staff as the valuable resources of the company.

These values became the focus of internal discussion and
communication. Many of the staff had picked them up
implicitly, and referred to 'the Concorde Way' when they
were talking about how the company functioned. They were
very proud of working for Concorde, and felt that it was
quite different from other organizations in a similar line of
work. They also felt confident that it would continue to grow
and develop in the future, and that they were lucky to work
there. As the management began to articulate its values

clearly in communication with the staff, this pride developed a clear focus and became a major, though internalized, force which shaped how the company's employees interacted with one another and with outsiders.

The consultancy reports for this company didn't recommend that the directors change what they were already doing. Rather, they identified their good management practices and highlighted their value, so that the directors could be more aware of them, and could continue to maintain their existing policies. As a result, the values of high-quality work and professional commitment became something which the directors could virtually take for granted among the staff. The company's employees became just as concerned as the directors to make sure that these values were reflected in their work and they were vigilant in making sure that the values were translated into their working practice.

(Source: Hayes and Lemon 1990)

take a policy decision to turn over to a team-working approach don't bother thinking the whole idea through. Changing a whole organization over to a team structure is very different from establishing a few specific task teams. It involves changes right across the board. It involves changes to the authority structures which operate within the organization, since teams have to have some opportunity for self-direction. It also involves changes to the established work structures in the organization, since effective and well-constructed teams will have expertise which is drawn from right across the existing departments or divisions.

In addition, changing to teamworking involves changes to the reward structures within an organization, since these traditionally operate purely on an individual basis while the team as a whole shares both responsibilities and failures. As we saw in Chapter 5, individual contributions do need to be acknowledged, in order to head off social loafing; but it is equally important that the team as a whole is recognized and its achievements rewarded. Changing to teamworking also involves adjusting the opportunity structures within the organization. Promotion systems based on seniority or individual experience have to give way to promotion systems which recognize teamworking and the development of team skills.

In other words, shifting an organization across to a fully team-work-based structure is in itself a radical, even revolutionary, challenge. As we have seen, it is one which can pay off dramatically, but Hackman argues strongly that it isn't a change which an organization should undertake without senior management thinking through all of the implications and considering whether they are really prepared to support and resource it fully.

FACTORS IN TEAM SUCCESS

Through this book, we have been looking at the kind of factors which can produce successful teams: teams which will make a positive contribution to their organizations. We have identified a number of different factors which can contribute to team success and explored a number of psychological mechanisms and processes which can help us to understand why teams produce the effects that they do.

When we analyse the factors involved in successful teams, we find that they can be summarized into three groups: accountability, opportunity and commitment. The team as a whole needs to be accountable to its organization – it must have a specific task or specific goals and it must be able to respond when asked to demonstrate how it has achieved them. The team also needs to have the opportunity to carry out its work: it must have the resources, the time and the skills or training which it will need, as well as having the ability to make the necessary decisions and implement them. And the team also needs commitment: both on the part of its own members to the team and on the part of the organization within which it is working.

When these factors are all present, we find that teamworking is able to draw on some very deep psychological motives and processes, which make it a rewarding experience for those who are participating in it. These psychological processes take many forms. Working in teams empowers people and helps them to develop an internal locus of control, which gives deeper work satisfaction and much less stress. It also enhances people's sense of self-efficacy, as they find themselves challenged to new levels of responsibility and achievement.

But perhaps the most significant of all the psychological processes going on in teamwork is the way that it encourages positive social identification – not just with the team itself, but also with the organization to which that team belongs. Teamworking encourages people to feel proud of belonging to their organization and of the contribution which they can make. And that, more than anything else, motivates all of us to do the best possible work that we can.

SUMMARY

- Teams can be a positive force for change in their organizations. The factors which encourage this are vision, participative safety, a climate for excellence and organizational support for innovation.
- Even though a team may only be a small part of an organization, psychological research has shown that minorities can be extremely influential, as long as they are consistent and autonomous.
- Teams need clear vision, effective communication, flexibility, persistence and a commitment to participation if they are to act as innovative forces within their organizations.
- Organizational resistance to teams may come from failure to understand the concept of a 'team', from personal discomfort with shared responsibility and from reluctance to implement organizational change.
- Factors which inhibit effective team performance include lack of autonomy, teams being too large, teams lacking support, commitment or resources, competitive appraisal systems, and a failure to provide feedback or acknowledgement.
- Introducing an organization to teamworking can involve a number of pitfalls, or 'trip-wires', for the management of the organization. These range from interacting with team members on an individual basis, to exerting too much or too little authority over the team.
- Essential factors in team success can be summarized as being about accountability, opportunity and commitment: the team needs to be accountable to its organization, it needs to have the opportunity to act effectively and it needs to be committed to what it is doing.

Box 7.4   **Management recommendations**

Investigate the realities of participative safety within the organization, by examining how managers really respond to employees who have critical views of management strategy.

Evaluate the team members' performance criteria critically to ensure that they do actually provide ways of rewarding dynamic and innovative approaches to work.

Ensure that the full implications of a teamworking approach have been considered by management and that the organization is really prepared to allow teams the bounded autonomy that they will require to act effectively.

Set up training days and other learning experiences which will help employees to learn how to act as team members rather than just as individuals. Be prepared to engage in personal coaching on this issue.

Use the six performance-inhibiting factors listed in Table 7.3 as a checklist to review the team's working conditions.

8 *Summary and conclusions*

SUMMARY

Successful team management, like any other form of management, is a complex affair. There are no simple rules that guarantee success, or magic guidelines which will always result in social harmony and high productivity. Human beings just aren't like that. But there are, none the less, a number of principles and concepts underlying team management which give a would-be manager a reasonable chance of success. And it is these which we have been exploring in this book. Perhaps it is worth just summarizing the main points of each chapter, before we try to bring it all together.

Why use teams?

Teams have a great deal of potential to contribute to modern organizational life. Part of that potential lies in their diversity and the hidden human resources which teamworking can uncover. Working teams encourage flexibility, involvement and efficiency, to the point where the introduction of teamworking has been known to transform companies entirely.

There are many different types of team and each type has its own distinctive characteristics and its own requirement. In addition, each team is made up of individuals, and there are millions of those. And for this reason, introducing teamworking as a mechanical, automated process is unlikely to be successful. People rarely respond well to being treated mechanistically and part of the strength and value of teamworking is being able to tap into individual insights and unique perceptions. Both Japanese and

Western firms have established cultures in which employee involvement is fostered and those individual insights are able to enrich the organization; but the process requires a certain amount of respect for individuality, as well as belief in the value of teamworking as a process.

The two mechanisms of social identification and social representations are both active psychological processes underlying successful teamwork. Social identification has to do with 'belonging' to a group and social representation has to do with sharing fundamental assumptions or beliefs of the group. Feeling proud of one's team or department and regarding it as special is intrinsically motivating for people and does not require conflict or competition with other groups to be effective. And managerial beliefs as well as organizational cultures can be seen as social representations, which exert considerable influence – not to mention power – over organizational life.

The team and the group

A team is fundamentally different from a working group. Teams are task-oriented and composed of people with different, but complementary, knowledge and skills. None the less, teams share many characteristics with working groups, such as the development of group norms, which help to define the team and keep it functioning smoothly and appropriately. Team norms tend to be more task-focused than the norms of ordinary working groups, though. Group cohesion is an important factor in teamworking and it can be seen as deriving from the human tendency for social identification, with both formal and informal communication playing an important part in establishing cohesion.

In some teams and working groups, their membership is signalled by visible signs such as specialized clothing. Their influence, however, is mainly concerned with the way that outsiders view team members and is less likely to contribute to a sense of belonging among the members themselves. Effective communication is the real factor which maintains group cohesion, but this can become problematic if the team members have very different personal construct systems. Personal constructs are our unique and personal ways of interpreting and making sense of information, and differences in personal constructs can produce misunderstandings or failures of communication.

A great deal of organizational research has focused on team roles, reflecting a more task-focused approach than earlier research into group roles. However, a weakness of the role approach in general is that it tends to ignore the transactional and interactional dimensions of people's behaviour. Other researchers have emphasized team skills, which tend to fall into three groups: those relating to technical or functional expertise, those to do with effective problem-solving and those to do with interpersonal interaction and social harmony. In many cases, though, team roles are less important than rigid organizational status distinctions, which can present a serious barrier to effective team working. Consequently, organizations which have adopted a team-working approach often try to minimize the trappings and signals of status.

Building a team

Building a team involves acting within the organization as a whole, to create a situation where the team members are able to act effectively. Four main approaches to team-building can be detected in the organizational literature: the interpersonal approach, the role-definition approach, the values approach and the task-oriented approach; and the chapter ends with a fifth: the social identity approach.

The interpersonal approach emphasizes the way that the team members interact with one another. Team-building using this model aims to ensure that the team members can interact at an honest, personal level. The role-definition approach draws on various typologies of roles and group processes and aims to make individuals aware of the style of contribution which they make in discussions. It also aims to make teams aware of particular types of contribution which may be missing from their working practices. The values approach, on the other hand, emphasizes the importance of the team having a clearly articulated set of values. These values need to be shared by all of the team's members, so that they can direct and inform each individual's actions in a coherent and co-ordinated way.

The task-oriented approach to team-building focuses on the skills and resources which the team needs to develop or assemble in order to tackle its task effectively. Interpersonal relationships, the establishment of common goals and team values are regarded as part of the required tools for effective task completion. The social identity approach to team-building incorporates many of the insights of the other approaches and does not aim to contradict them. Instead, it focuses on developing a strong sense of team identification through establishing clear team boundaries, promoting cohesion through effective communication and encouraging pride in the team through achievement and through professionalization.

The team and its leader

A team's leader operates within the team to ensure that it works with clarity and direction, whereas a team's manager is outside the team, but facilitates the team's operations by making resources available and setting targets. Both the leader and the manager undertake some aspects of the leadership role.

Leadership beliefs can result in self-fulfilling prophecies, which can influence how employees behave. Theories of leadership have included trait theories, situational theories, attributional approaches, contingency models, transactional theories and transformational approaches. In addition, various types of power operating within organizations have been identified which can be roughly classified into power which derives from the person's position within an organization and power which derives from the individual's personal characteristics. Understanding how power works in organizations is relevant for successful team management because empowerment is such an important concept in teamworking, and requires a management philosophy which assumes that day-to-day decisions about work are best undertaken by those who are doing that work.

There has been some debate about how necessary leaders really are, but the consensus is that although teams can take on a great deal of autonomy, they need leaders to give them direction and to keep them targeted on their work. The main principles of team leadership include keeping the goals clear, building confidence, commitment and skills, managing external relationships, creating opportunities for team members and doing real work. They draw on the underlying psychological mechanisms of social identification, by encouraging cohesion between group members, establishing a sense of professionalism or working competence and so allowing people to identify with their team and feel proud of belonging to it.

Evaluating team performance

Psychometric approaches to team measurement have included the Belbin Team Role Self-Perception Inventory and specialized scoring systems for the 16PF and OPQ. However, it has been argued that assessments of team role may not take account of more subtle aspects of team functioning. The Team Climate Inventory locates team functioning in its organizational context and looks at the relationship between organizational innovation and teamworking in terms of four dimensions: participative safety, support for innovation, vision and task orientation. By contrast, however, Katzenbach and Smith proposed evaluating team performance by using themes and identity, enthusiasm and energy, event-driven histories, personal commitment and performance results to identify where a team would fall on their team performance curve.

Psychological research into the cognitive aspects of group decision-making highlighted two important cognitive mechanisms which can distort the quality of the decisions made by teams. One of these is group polarization, which is the tendency of groups to make more extreme decisions than the same individuals would make if they were acting on their own. The second is groupthink, which is the tendency for highly cohesive groups to become self-centred and divorced from reality. This leads them to make unrealistic and sometimes disastrous decisions and is only challenged by cultivating dissent. However, some teams oppose groupthink by cultivating teamthink, which involves positive thinking styles and is particularly influenced by the self-efficacy beliefs held by team members.

Social loafing is another process which can result in a lowering of team performance and it needs to be challenged by ensuring that individual efforts can always be recognized. As a result, team reward systems which do not also recognize individual contributions can be counter-productive, although team rewards can work alongside individual ones to promote social identification with the team. Sanctions, whether individual or team-based have been shown (yet again) to be less effective than rewards in encouraging positive contributions to teamworking.

The team in its organization

Research has shown that the way that teams interact with their organizations can be vital for their effectiveness or for their success. This interaction can take many different forms, and does not just involve the team's leader. At the same time, organizational support for teamwork is essential. Organizations which are supportive of teamwork often have a relatively 'flat' shape and a culture which includes trust and confidence in employees – it is more difficult for hierarchical organizations to empower teamworkers effectively.

Theories of organizational culture range from typologies, semiotic, and systems analyses to the view of culture as fundamental shared beliefs. The current model is layered, with a manifest level of symbols and other signs, a strategic level of distinctive practices and a core level of deeply-held beliefs and assumptions. It may also be useful to see organizational cultures as networks of working groups, teams and departments, each of which shares the organization's culture to a greater or lesser degree. This approach highlights the importance of social identification as an underlying psychological process and also the role of teams and working groups in maintaining the organization's culture.

Competition between teams has to be carefully managed so as to ensure that it is competition about achievement rather than competition about organizational resources. The one can promote positive, friendly rivalry, while the other merely promotes political manoevering and intergroup hostility. Teams can be a major force in organizational change, partly because their own approaches and values can represent positive directions for change and partly through the way that they interact with the organization as a whole. But if they are to function effectively, teams also require organizational support, in the form of clear targets, adequate resources, reliable information, training and education, regular feedback and technical or process assistance.

Teams, organizations and innovation

Teams can be powerful forces for innovation in their organizations. The factors which encourage this are vision, participative safety, a climate for excellence and organizational support for innovation. Even though a team may only be a small part of an organization, psychological research has shown that minorities can be extremely influential, as long as they are consistent and autonomous. But teams need clear vision, effective communication, flexibility, persistence and a commitment to participation if they are to act as innovative forces within their organizations.

Organizational resistance to teams does occur and can come from three sources: failure to understand the concept of a 'team', personal discomfort with shared responsibility, or an underlying reluctance to implement organizational change. Hackman argued that there are a number of pitfalls, or 'trip-wires', which can interfere with the process of changing over an organization to teamworking. These range from the organization insisting on interacting with team members on an individual basis and not as a team, to that organization exerting either too much or too little authority over the team.

Essential factors in team success can be summarized as being about accountability, opportunity and commitment: the team needs to be accountable to its organization, it needs to have the opportunity to act effectively and it needs to be committed to what it is doing. But team performance will be inhibited by lack of autonomy, teams being too large, teams lacking support, commitment or resources, competitive appraisal systems and a failure to provide feedback or acknowledgement.

WHAT CAN TEAM MANAGERS DO?

The management recommendations at the end of each chapter in the book have included a number of practical recommendations for team managers. It is essential to provide the team with the resources that it will need – including dedicated time for team-building and other activities. It is important to establish communication mechanisms, not just within the team but also between the team and the rest of the organization. And it is necessary to make sure that the team is able to obtain the expertise which it needs: either through training or through establishing effective liaison with the appropriate specialists. But this is just a summary: as the reader will have seen, there are many more detailed recommendations at the end of each chapter in this book.

What is particularly important for a team manager, though, is to make sure that all the necessary conditions for positive social identification within the team are in place. The best way to think of this is in terms of the three features of social identification: boundaries, cohesion and self-esteem. It is vital that each team has a clear sense of their boundaries and this should not be left to evolve by itself, in case the boundaries appear in the wrong place and the team becomes hampered by factionalism and in-fighting. It is up to the team manager to establish conditions whereby each team has a clear definition of itself and a clear sense of the part that it plays in the wider organization.

The team manager also needs to make sure that the communication mechanisms which will promote effective team cohesion are in place. That communication can (indeed, should) be both formal and informal; it can be about the organization as a whole or the department as well as about the team and it should ensure that team members understand each others' roles and specialisms as well as the task demands and organizational contexts within which they are working. It also needs to work in all direction: one-way communication mechanisms simply won't serve the purpose.

In particular, the team manager needs to foster a sense of pride in belonging to the team and in working for the organization. That can happen in many ways: through emphasizing achievements, through building high professional standards, through encouraging positive customer care, or all three and some others besides. But it is an important part of the team manager's job to ensure that people are able to feel proud of belonging to their team. In this way, the manager will be able to harness the psychological processes of social identification, to aid and amplify teamworking.

WHAT CAN DIRECTORS DO?

The hands-on aspects of team management don't really apply to high-level management, which is more likely to be involved at the level of policy and strategic decision-making. But as we have seen throughout this book, without support at the higher levels of the organization, teamworking is unlikely to become particularly successful. High level management needs to provide the vision, the strategy and the resources to make teamworking work.

Many of the management recommendations at the end of each chapter in this book are really in the province of higher management. They are concerned with organizational issues, rather than with the practical concerns of the team manager. Some, for example, are about the whole organizational ethos, including features such as status distinctions, reorganization to remove obstructive organizational systems, reward criteria, empowerment and so on. They carry a vital message: that high-level management needs to spend some time working out the organizational support team-working will need, if it is to achieve the productive synergy which can so transform an organization.

Directors and high-level management, too, can benefit from keeping social identity processes in mind. It is they who can provide the content of communications which will help employees to feel proud of the organization's achievements. It is they who can establish the resources for building professionalism and customer care into daily work. And it is they who can ensure that the organization has a definite, positive direction, with clearly delineated values which are understood and shared by all of its members.

It is possible, of course, for teams to operate with departmental support alone. Team managers can achieve a great deal to promote co-operative and mutually productive working. But teams working in that way are unlikely to achieve the powerful synergy and dynamism of their potential. They need active consideration and help from high-level management, as well as from their own line managers.

Most importantly of all, perhaps, directors could use the principles in this book to examine their own ways of working. The high-level management of an organization is generally referred to as a team, but too often we find that it really works as a collection of individuals, each with a separate agenda and little shared vision. Spending time working on the characteristics of the team, and in particular on developing a shared vision and an atmosphere of participative safety, is always time well spent.

CONCLUSIONS

Team management, then, is complex but it is not chaotic. I hope that this book has enabled the reader to come to terms with some of that complexity and to understand some of the issues and points of view involved in successful team management. Human beings

are all different, as is each organization, so each researcher ends
up with their own particular view drawn from their own particular
experience. And it is this which leads to the complexity. But if we
sift through all that detail, we can detect just a few fundamental
principles of team management which recur in different forms
over and over again. No matter where it is found, or which
particular model it follows, successful team management invariably encompasses these fundamental principles.

There are three of them altogether. The first, which I have been
at pains to point out as it recurs, is that of **social identification**.
This basic tendency in human beings – our need to classify the
world into 'them-and-us' groups – need not be destructive. It can
be harnessed positively, if the team's manager and leader are
sensitized to how it works and make sure that they establish the
three fundamental requirements: clear boundaries, effective communication to promote cohesion and, above all else, opportunities
for the team members to feel proud and special by belonging to
their team.

The second recurrent principle is to do with shared **beliefs**. In
the first chapter, I discussed the psychological cognitions known
as social representations and the way that these can be involved in
organizational life. Social representations, in one form or another,
have come up over and over again in this book: in the different
models and ways of understanding team-building; in the various
ideas about leadership and power and how they have influenced
teamworking practice; in the manifestations of groupthink and
teamthink; and in the ways that we understand organizational
culture. Realizing that social representations can vary from one
organization, division or department to another – or even from one
team to another – can help us to understand something of what is
going on as a team leader encourages a team to approach their task
in a positive, 'can-do-ish' way.

Perhaps the most important principle of all in successful team
management, though, is that of **respect**. The whole point of
teamworking is the way that it allows the organization to draw
on the thoughts, ideas and talents of the people that it employs.
And that can't happen unless the organization respects what those
people have to say. Team empowerment, providing autonomy in
decision-making, establishing opportunities for training, resourcing the team adequately and all the other aspects of organiza-

tional support for teamworking are, underneath it all, manifestations of respect. They arise from the team's management recognizing that they need to listen to what team members are saying and to take it seriously. People are quick to detect the difference between real respect and lip-service and they will respond appropriately. Trying to engage in successful team management without respect for the people who make up the teams is as pointless as trying to ski in flippers.

—— References

Adair, J. (1986) *Effective Team-building*, Gower, Farnborough.

Agrell, A. and Gustafson, R. (1994) The Team Climate Inventory (TCI) and group innovation: a psychometric test on a Swedish sample of work groups. *Journal of Occupational and Organizational Psychology*, **67**. pp. 143–51.

Ancona, D. G. and Caldwell, D. F. (1988) Beyond task and maintenance: defining external functions in groups. *Group and Organization Studies*, **13**, pp. 468–94.

Ancona, D. G. and Caldwell, D. F. (1990) Beyond boundary spanning: managing external dependence in product management teams. *Journal of High Technology Management Research*, **1**, pp. 119–35.

Ancona, D. G. and Caldwell, D. F. (1992) Bridging the boundary: external activity and performance in organizational teams. *Administrative Science Quarterly*, **37**, pp. 634–65.

Anderson, N.R., Hardy, G. and West, M.A. (1990) Innovative teams at work. *Personnel Management*, **22(9)**, pp. 48–53.

Anderson, N. R. and West, M. A. (1994a) *The Team Climate Inventory: Manual and User's Guide*, ASE, NFER-Nelson, Windsor.

Anderson, N. R. and West, M. A. (1994b) *Team Climate: Measuring and Predicting Innovation in Groups at Work*. Paper presented at the BPS Occupational Psychology Conference, Birmingham, UK.

Anderson, N. R. and West, M. A. (1996) The Team Climate Inventory: development of the TCI and its application in teambuilding for innovativeness. *European Journal of Work and Organizational Psychology*, **5(1)**, pp. 53–66.

Asch, S. E. (1956) Studies of independence and conformity: a minority of one against a unanimous majority. *Psychological Monographs*, **70** No 9.

Ashforth, B. E. and Mael, F. (1989) Social Identity theory and the organization. *Academy of Management Review*, **14**, pp. 20–39.

Baker, D. P. and Salas, E. (1992) Principles for measuring teamwork skills. *Human Factors*, **34(4)**, pp. 469–75.

Bales, R. F. (1950) *Interaction Process Analysis*, Addison-Wesley, Cambridge, Mass.

Bandura, A. (1989) Perceived self-efficacy in the exercise of personal agency. *The Psychologist*, **2**, pp. 411–24.

Belbin, R. M. (1981) *Management Teams*, Heinemann, London.

Belbin, R. M. (1993a) A reply to the Belbin Team-Role Self-Perception Inventory by Furnham, Steele and Pendleton. *Journal of Occupational and Organizational Psychology*, **66**, pp. 259–60.

Belbin, R. M. (1993b) *Team Roles at Work*, Butterworth Heinemann, Oxford.

Belbin Associates (1988) *Interplace: Matching People to Jobs*, Belbin Associates, Cambridge.

Benne, K. D. and Sheats, P. (1948) Functional Group Members. *Journal of Social Issues*, **4**, pp. 41–9.

Bennis, W. (1966) *Changing Organizations*, McGraw Hill, New York.

Berne, E. (1973) *Games People Play*, Penguin, Harmondsworth.

Bower, D. G. (1994) Rover's Return: culture, process and organizational change in the Rover Group. *The Occupational Psychologist*, **23**, pp. 9–19.

Buller, P. F. and Bell, C. H. Jr. (1986) Effects of team-building and goal setting on productivity: a field experiment. *Academy of Management Journal*, **29**, pp. 305–28.

Davis, T. R. V. (1985) Managing culture at the bottom, in *Gaining Control of the Corporate Culture* (eds. Killman *et al.*) Jossey-Bass, San Francisco.

Deci, E. L. (1971) Effects of externally mediated rewards on intrinsic motivation. *Journal of Applied Psychology*, **18**, pp. 105–15

Dulewicz, V. (1995) A validation of Belbin's team roles from 16PF and OPQ using bosses' ratings of competence. *Journal of Occupational and Organizational Psychology*, **68**, pp. 81–99.

Dyer, J. L. (1984) Team research and training: a state of the art review. *Human Factors Review*, pp. 285–323.

Feldman, D. C. (1984) The development and enforcement of group norms. *Academy of Management Review*, January, pp. 47–53.

Fiedler, F. E. (1967) *A Theory of Leadership Effectiveness*, McGraw Hill, New York.

French, J. R. P. and Raven, B. (1959) The bases of power, in *Studies in social power* (ed. D.Cartwright) University of Michigan, Ann Arbor.

Furnham, A., Steele, H. and Pendleton, D. (1993a) A psychometric assessment of the Belbin Team-Role Self-Perception Inventory. *Journal of Occupational and Organizational Psychology*, **66**, pp. 245–57.

Furnham, A., Steele, H. and Pendleton, D. (1993b) A Response to Dr. Belbin's reply. *Journal of Occupational and Organizational Psychology*, **66**, pp. 261.

Gaertner, K. N. and Nollen, S. D. (1992) Turnover intentions and desire among executives. *Human Relations*, **45(5)**, pp. 447–65.

George, J. M. (1992) Intrinsic and extrinsic origins of perceived social loafing in organizations. *Academy of Management Journal*, **35**, pp. 191–202.

George, J. M. (1995) Asymmetrical effects of rewards and punishments: the case of social loafing. *Journal of Occupational and Organizational Psychology*, **68**, pp. 327–38.

Gladstein, D. L. (1984) Groups in context: a model of task group effectiveness. *Administrative Science Quarterly*, **29**, pp. 499–517.

Glover, H. D. (1992) Organisational change and development: the consequences of misuse. *Leadership and Organization Development Journal*, **13(1)**, pp. 9–16.

Graen, G. (1975) Role-making processes within complex organizations, in *Handbook of Industrial and Organizational Psychology* (ed. M. D. Dunnette) Jossey-Bass, San Francisco.

Greene, C. N. and Podsakoff, P. M. (1981) Effects of withdrawal of performance-contingent reward on supervisory influence and power. *Academy of Management Journal*, **24**, pp. 527–42.

Guest, D. (1995) *New Perspectives in Organisational Development: A Theoretical Overview*. BPS Occupational Psychology Division conference 'New Perspectives in Organisational Development', September 1995, London.

Hackman, J. R. (1994) Trip wires in designing and leading workgroups. *The Occupational Psychologist*, **23**, pp. 3–8.

Hackman, J. R. (ed.) (1990) *Groups that Work (and those that don't): Conditions for Effective Teamwork*, Jossey Bass, San Francisco.

Harkins, S. and Jackson, J. (1985) The role of evaluation in eliminating social loafing. *Personality and Social Psychology Bulletin*, **11**, pp. 457–65.

Harrison, R. (1972a) When power conflicts trigger team spirit. *European Business*, Spring, pp. 27–65.

Harrison, R. (1972b) Understanding your organization's culture. *Harvard Business Review*, **50(23)**, pp. 119–28.

Hayes, N. J. (1991) Social identity, social representations and organizational culture. PhD Thesis CNAA / Huddersfield Polytechnic.

Hayes, N. J. and Lemon, N. (1990) Stimulating Positive Cultures in Growing Companies. *Leadership and Organisational Change Management*, **11(7)**, 17–21.

Hodgetts, R. M. (1991) *Organisational behaviour: theory and practice*, Macmillan, New York.

Hogg, M. A. and Abrams, D. (1993) Towards a single-process uncertainty-reduction model of social motivation in groups, in *Group Motivation: Social Psychological Perspectives* (eds M.A.Hogg and D. Abrams) Harvester Wheatsheaf, London.

Hollander, E. P. (1958) Conformity, status and idiosyncrasy credit. *Psychological Review*, **65**, pp. 117–27.

Hollander, E. P. and Julian, J. W. (1978) A further look at leader legitimacy, influence and innovation, in *Group Processes* (ed. L. Berkowitz) Academic Press, New York.

Hollander, E. P. and Offerman, L. R. (1990) Power and leadership in organizations: relationships in transition. *American Psychologist*, **45**, pp. 179–89.

House, R. J. (1971) A path-goal theory of leader effectiveness. *Administrative Science Quarterly*, **16**, pp. 321–38.

Ibbetson, A. and Newell, S. (1995) *Winner takes all: an evaluation of adventure-based management training.* Paper delivered at the BPS Occupational Psychology Conference, January 1995, Warwick, UK.

Imai, M. (1986) *Kaizen: the Key to Japan's Competitive Success*, Random House, New York.

Janis, I. L. (1972) *Victims of Groupthink*, Houghton Mifflin, Boston.

Janis, I. L. (1983) The role of social support in adherence to stressful decisions. *American Psychologist*, **38**, pp. 143–60.

Jodelet, D. (1991) *Madness and Social Representations* (trans. T. Powell), Harvester Wheatsheaf, Hemel Hempstead.

Johnson, C., Wood, R. and Blinkhorn, S. (1988) Spuriouser and spuriouser: the use of ipsative personality tests. *Journal of Occupational Psychology*, **61**, pp. 153–61.

Kanter, R. M. (1983) *The Change Masters: Corporate Entrepreneurs at Work*, George Allen and Unwin, London.

Kaplan, R. E. (1986) Is openness passé? *Human Relations*, **39(3)**, pp. 229–43.

Katzenbach, J. R. and Smith, D. K. (1993) *The Wisdom of Teams: Creating the High-performance Organization*, Harvard Business School Press, Boston, Mass.

Keller, R. T. (1986) Predictors of the performance of project groups in research and development organizations. *Academy of Management Review*, December, pp. 715–26.

Kelly, G. (1955) *The Theory of Personal Constructs*, Norton, New York.

King, N. and Anderson, N. (1995) *Innovation and change in organizations*, ITBP, London.

Kipnis, D. (1976) *The Powerholders*, University of Chicago Press, Chicago.

Laiken, M. E. (1994) The myth of the self-managing team. *Organization Development Journal*, **12(2)**, pp. 29–34.

Latané, B., Williams, K. and Harkins, S. (1979) Many hands make light work: the causes and consequences of social loafing. *Journal of Personality and Social Psychology*, **37**, pp. 822–32.

Lea, M. and Spears, R. (19910 Computer-mediated communication, deindividuation and group decision-making. *International Journal of Man Machine Studies*, **34**, pp. 283–301.

Lewin, K., Lippitt, R. and White, R. K. (1939) Patterns of aggressive behaviour in artificially created social climates. *Journal of Social Psychology*, **10**, pp. 271–99.

Liden, R. C. and Graen, G. (1980) Generalisability of the vertical dyad linkage model of leadership. *Academy of Management Journal*, **23**, pp. 451–65.

Likert, R. (1967) *The Human Organisation: Its Management and Value*, McGraw Hill, Tokyo.

Locke, E. A., Shaw, K. N., Saari, L. M. and Latham, G. P. (1982) Goal setting and task performance: 1969–1980. *Psychological Bulletin*, **90**, pp. 125–52.

Lowin, A. and Craig, J. R. (1968) The influence of level of performance on managerial style: an experimental object-lesson in the ambiguity of correlational data. *Organizational Behaviour and Human Performance*, **3**, 440–58.

Lundberg, C. C. (1990) Surfacing organizational culture. *Journal of Managerial Psychology*, **5**, pp. 19–26.

Mabey, W. and Hunter, R. (1986) Using personality measures to improve selection. *Guidance & Assessment Review*, **2(5)**, pp. 1–4.

Manz, C. C. (1992) Self-leading work teams: moving beyond self-management myths. *Human Relations*, **45(11)**, pp. 1119–40.

Manz, C. C. and Sims, H. P. Jr (1982) The potential for groupthink in autonomous work groups. *Human Relations*, **35**, pp. 773-84.

Margerison, C. J. and McCann, D. (1991) *Team Management: Practical Approaches*, Mercury Books, London.

Marques, J. M. and Yzerbyt, V. Y. (1988) The black sheep effect: judgemental extremity towards ingroup members in inter and intra group situations. *European Journal of Social Psychology*, **18**, pp. 287–92.

Mayo, E. (1933) *The Human Problems of an Industrial Civilisation*, Macmillan, London.

McGregor, D. (1960) *The Human Side of Enterprise*, McGraw Hill, New York.

McKenna, E. (1994) *Business Psychology and Organisational Behaviour: a students' handbook*, Lawrence Erlbaum Associates, Hove.

Meindl, J. R. (1992) Reinventing leadership: a radical, social psychological approach, in *Social Psychology in Organisations: Advances in Theory and Research* (ed. K. Murnigham) Prentice-Hall, Englewood Cliffs, N.J.

Meindl, J. R. and Ehrlich, S. B. (1987) The romance of leadership and the evaluation of organizational performance. *Academy of Management Journal*, **30(1)**, pp. 91–109.

Moorhead, G., Ference, R. and Neck, C. P. (1991) Group decision fiascoes continue: space shuttle Challenger and a revised groupthink framework. *Human Relations*, **44(6)**, pp. 539–50.

Moscovici, S. (1984) The phenomenon of social representations, in *Social Representations* (eds R. M. Farr and S. Moscovici) Cambridge University Press, Cambridge.

Moscovici, S. and Lage, E. (1976) Studies in social influence III: majority vs minority influence in a group. *European Journal of Social Psychology*, **6**, pp. 149–74.

Moscovici, S. and Zavalloni, M. (1969) The group as a polariser of attitude. *Journal of Personality & Social Psychology*, **12**, pp. 125–35.

Mummendey, A. and Schreiber, H. J. (1984) Social comparison, similarity and ingroup favouritism: A replication. *European Journal of Social Psychology*, **14**, pp. 231–33.

Neck, C. P. and Manz, C. C. (1994) From groupthink to teamthink: toward the creation of constructive thought patterns in self-managing work teams. *Human Relations*, **47(8)**, pp. 929–52.

Nemeth, C. and Wachtler, J. (1974) Creating the perceptions of consistency and confidence: a necessary condition for minority influence. *Sociometry*, **37**, pp. 529–40.

Perez, J. A. and Mugny, G. (1987) Paradoxical effects of categorization in minority influence: when being an outgroup is an advantage. *European Journal of Social Psychology*, **17**, pp. 157–69.

Perrin, S. and Spencer, C. (1980) The Asch effect: a child of its time? *Bulletin of the British Psychological Society*, **32**, pp. 405–6.

Peters, T. J. (1978) Symbols, patterns and settings: an optimistic case for getting things done. *Organisational Dynamics*, **7**, pp. 2–23.

Peters, T. L. and Waterman, R. H. (1982) *In Search of Excellence: Lessons from America's Best-run Companies*, Harper and Row, New York.

Piper, W. E., Marrache, M. Lacroix, R., Richardson, A. M. and Jones, B. D. (1983) Cohesion as a basic bond in groups. *Human Relations*, February, pp. 93–108.

Podsakoff, P. M. and Schriesheim, C. A. (1985) Field studies of French and Raven's bases of power: critique, reanalysis and suggestions for future research. *Psychological Bulletin*, **97(3)**, pp. 387–411.

Robinson, D. and Hayes, N. J. (1994) *Social identity and social representations in user-centred design*. Paper delivered at the 23rd International Congress of Applied Psychology, July 1994, Madrid.

Roesthlisberger, F. J. and Dickson, W. J. (1949) *Management and the Worker*, Harvard University Press, Cambridge, Mass.

Rogers, C. R. (1961) *On Becoming a Person: A Therapist's View of Psychotherapy*, Constable, London.

Rosenthal, R. and Fode, K. L. (1963) The effect of experimenter bias on the performance of the albino rat. *Behavioural Science*, **8**, pp. 183–9.

Rosenthal, R. and Jacobsen, L. (1968) *Pygmalian in the Classroom: Teacher Expectations and Pupil Intellectual Development*, Holt, Rinehart and Winston, New York.

Schein, E. H. (1985) *Organisational Culture and Leadership: A Dynamic View*, Jossey-Bass, San Francisco.

Schein, E. H. (1988) *Process Consultation: Its Role in Organizational Development Vol 1*, Addison-Wesley, Reading, Mass.

Schein, E. H. (1990) Organisational Culture. *American Psychologist* , **45**, pp. 109–19.

Shackleton, V. (1995) *Business Leadership*, Routledge, London.

Shea, G. P. (1986) Quality circles: the danger of bottled change. *Sloan Management Review*, **27**, pp. 33–46.

Shipper, F. and Manz, C. C. (1992) Employee self-management without formally designated teams: an alternative road to empowerment. *Organizational Dynamics*, **20(3)**, pp. 48–61.

Silverman, I. (1977) *The Human Subject in the Psychological Laboratory*, Pergamon, Oxford.

Smith, P. B. and Peterson, M. F. (1988) *Leadership, Organizations and Culture*, Sage, London.

Stoner, J. A. F. (1961) A comparison of individual and group decisions involving risk. Masters thesis, MIT School of Industrial Management.

Sundstrom, E., de Meuse, K. P. and Futrell, D. (1990) Work teams: applications and effectiveness. *American Psychologist*, **45**, pp. 120–33.

Tajfel, H. and Turner, J. C. (1979) An Integrative Theory of Intergroup Conflict in *The Social Psychology of Intergroup Relations* (eds W. G. Austin and S. Worchel) Brooks/Cole, Monterey, Cal.

Tajfel, H. and Wilkes, A. L. (1963) Classification and quantitative judgement. *British Journal of Psychology*, **54**, pp. 101–14.

Thomsett, R. (1980) *People and Project Management*, Yourdon Press, New York.

Triplett, N. (1988) Dynamogenic factors in pacemaking and competition. *American Journal of Psychology*, **9**, pp. 507–33.

Van Maanen, J. and Barley, S. R. (1985) Cultural organization: fragments of a theory, in *Organisational Culture* (eds P. J. Frost *et al.*) Sage, London.

Venkatesan, M. (1966) Experimental study of consumer behaviour conformity and independence. *Journal of Marketing Research*, **3**, pp. 384–7.

Vroom, V. H. and Yetton, P. W. (1973) *Leadership and decision-making*, University of Pittsburgh Press, Pittsburgh, PA.

West, M. A. (1990) The social psychology of work group innovation, in *Innovation and Creativity at Work: Psychological and Organizational Strategies* (eds M.A. West and J. L. Farr) Wiley, London.

West, M. A. (1994) *Effective Teamwork*, BPS Books, Leicester.

West, M. A. and Wallace, M. (1991) Innovation in health care teams. *European Journal of Social Psychology*, **21**, pp. 303–15.

Yukl, G. A. and Falbe, C. M. (1991) Importance of different power sources in downward and lateral relations. *Journal of Applied Psychology*, **76**, pp. 416–23.

Index

Adair, J. 53
Agrell, A. and Gustafson, R. 124–5
Ancona, D.G. and Caldwell, D.F.
  149–52
Anderson, N.R., *et al.* 183, 186; and
  West, M.A. 124, 126
Asch, S.E. 34
Ashforth, B.E. and Mael, F. 163

Baker, D.P. and Salas, E. 122–3
Bales, R.F. 70
Bandura, A. 139
Belbin Associates 119
Belbin, R.M. 47, 48, 51, 52, 71,
  118–20, 121
Belbin Team Role Self-Perception
  Inventory (BTRSPI) 118–20, 146
Benne, K.D. and Sheats, P. 44–5, 69
Bennis, W. 61
Berne, E. 65–6
Bower, D.G. 13
Buller, P.F. and Bell, C.H. 77

cohesion 36–8, 55, 114, 116, 210;
  clothing 39–41; communication
  41–2, 44; team 38–9
communication 41–2, 44, 81, 83, 167,
  210
culture *see* organizational culture

Davis, T.R.V. 169, 174
Deci, E.L. 143–4
decision-making 131, 146–7;

groupthink 133–8; polarization
  131–3, 213; teamthink 138–40
directors 216–17
Dulewicz, V. 121, 122
Dyer, J.L. 122

empowerment 98–9, 115, 212, 218;
  boundaries 105; confidence 104;
  information 105; managing 104–6;
  power over, to and from 100–1; rates
  of progress 105–6; respect and belief
  104; and reward systems 99–100;
  and teamworking 101–4; training
  105
external activity 149–51; ambassador
  150, 151, 153–4; guard 150; scout
  150, 152; task co-ordinator 150,
  151–2

Feldman, D.C. 31, 32
French, J.R.P. and Raven, B. 98
Furnham, A. *et al.* 119–20

Gaertner, K.N. and Nollen, S.D. 166
George, J.M. 143–5
Gladstein, D.L. 148
Glover, H.D. 197
group norms 29, 54; changes to 29, 31;
  and conformity 34–5; functions of
  31–2; pivotal and peripheral 32–3, 35
groups 146; cohesion 36–8, 39–42, 54;
  described 210–11; polarization